Fig. 2: Helmet of Norfolk Rangers less crest and plume, c.1799.

Although the description of the headdress may be a little confusing, the opening paragraph from Tomkins's paper does give a description of the uniforms designed by Lord Townshend and the sound reasons for his choice.

'This Corps was first raised in the year 1782, and at that time consisted of a troop of cavalry, and a company of infantry, the whole under the command of the gallant Marquis Townshend. The singularity of their uniform, and the high state of their discipline, were equally objects of public attention, and are evincive proofs of the regard with which their veteran commandant views every minutiae of military preparation. Towards the close of the American war their uniform was green with black facings, and was well adapted to conceal their movements in woods or over forests. Their hats which were round, had a peg at the top fitted securely to the centre of the crown, and from which proceeded different chains as far as the neck, chest and shoulders, these chains appeared like radii from a centre, and, exclusive of the ingenuity of contrivance, were well constructed for warding off the stroke of a sabre from the head and neck. They carried but one pistol, but this was a double barrelled one, and was capable of being fitted with great facility to a but [sic] which hung from the right shoulder, by means of which they could take good aim at any opposed object. The other holster contained ammunition, and sufficiency of provision for one day.'

An initial meeting was held during May 1782 and duly reported in the *Norwich Mercury,* whilst on September 14th the following appeared in the same paper:– '----- on the Sunday morning, a very respectable body of gentlemen, farmers and tradesmen, waited on his Lordship as volunteers to serve in a corps (styled The Norfolk Rangers) in order to protect the county of Norfolk from any insults from the enemy. The Foot being upwards of fifty, were clothed in a genteel green uniform with black caps and green feathers, at his Lordship's expense; the Horse being more numerous, and cons[...] provide ther[...] er 26th:– 'Las[...] issued his Maj[...] ain of a corp[...] Norfolk Ran[...] s neigh- bour[...].' ('The abov[...] ious and unique appointment to a Captaincy, as Lord Townshend at the time was full Colonel of the 2nd Dragoon Guards and a Lieutenant-General in the army.' – Harvey's *Records.*)

In November first mention is made of any Permanent Staff of Instructors – drawn from his own Regiment, the 2nd Dragoon Guards, as well as the 20th Light Dragoons and the West Norfolk Militia. Exercises were carried out after the harvest of 1782 and a Rangers Ball was arranged for January 18th, 1783, at Rainham Hall.

Detailed evidence of the 1782/3 uniform can be gathered from a portrait dated 1783 of Sir Martin Browne Folkes, Bart., of Hillington Hall, Norfolk[3]:–

Headdress. Not shown in the portrait but would have been a Tarleton helmet with feather. (Photograph of an actual specimen reproduced in Harvey.)
Coat. A long coat of green material with black collar and cuffs piped white, and white piping down front of coat on both sides. Two rows of silver buttons each side of the opening of coat, cut back below the 4th button to show a white waistcoat. Gold fringed epaulettes on shoulders. Black stock at neck and showing white shirt frill at collar opening.
Shoulder-belt. White.
Shoulder-belt plate. Oval copper plate carrying a white metal shield with the letters N R below a crown, both in yellow metal.
Breeches. Not shown but would be white.
Boots. Black knee boots.

Fig. 3: Standard of the Holkham Yeomanry Cavalry 1798. Reproduced in full colour in Harvey's *Records.*

Helmet. Fur crested, an all white plume on right side of helmet and a green turban wound around, the latter kept in place by small white metal chains, white metal title band around the front. See Fig. 2.
Jacket. Green, black collar and cuffs edged white or silver, central single strand of silver on collar. Nine loops of silver lace across front visible, but probably twelve in all, three covered by waist sash. At collar a black stock with white shirt frill below. On shoulders, wings of white metal chain on black cloth edged silver.
Shoulder-belt. White.
Shoulder-belt plate. Oval with crown and N R as previously described.
Waist sash. Crimson.
Breeches. White.
Boots. Black knee boots.
Sword. Blade – section below hilt blue with gilt ornamentation.
Saddle. Brown leather with black sheepskin cover.
Bridle. Black.
Pistol holster. Black.
Valise. Black.

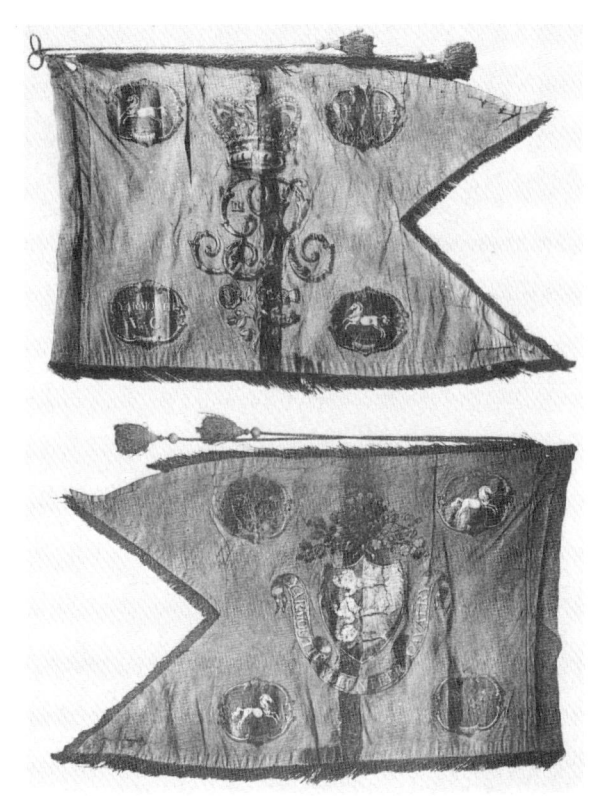

Fig. 4: Standard of the Yarmouth Volunteer Cavalry 1798. Reproduced from photograph in Harvey's *Records.*

Lord Orford's Troop of Norfolk Rangers wore a similar uniform as did Sir Edward Astley's Troop, from the Melton district, but the latter had orange facings.

*   *   *

Although in 1793 the Peace of Versailles was signed and the American War ended, the Rangers remained a corporate body and was probably inspected annually, one such inspection taking place at Rainham Hall is recorded for 29 September 1792.

The Norfolk Rangers
1794-1806: Second period

Resulting from the renewed outbreak of hostilities with France in 1793, it was announced during March 1794 that a Force to be known as the Yeomanry Cavalry was to be raised throughout the United Kingdom. Thus in 1794 his Lordship, although in his late 70s, again took command of his old Corps – The Norfolk Rangers, now enrolled as Yeomanry. (Lord Townshend was promoted Field Marshal 30 July 1796.) During the ten years of comparative inactivity, uniform, horse furniture and equipment has obviously deteriorated, so we find some alterations in the Ranger's dress. A fine coloured print showing Lord Townshend in the new style of dress was published on 1 December 1799 in *Tomkins's Volunteers* (Fig. 1). It shows the Tarleton helmet, and that the jacket was still green with black facings, details as follows:

Elsewhere we find in the County of Norfolk that the East Norfolk (Hingham) Corps had the precedence in the U.K. of No. 23, with the official date recorded in the Establishment Book as 31 May 1794 – the Norfolk Rangers being of course No. 1 – and a precedence No. 27 for the Mid-Norfolk (Clackclose) Corps, recorded on 5 June 1794. From then on further Troops were raised throughout the County during the eight year period before the Peace of April 1802. The War Office listed the following Troops for the County in 1799:

Attleborough Troop.
Blofield and South Walsham Troop.
Clackclose Troop.
East Dereham Troop
Urpingham and Eynesford Troop.
Freebridge Lynn Troop.
Freebridge and Smithdown Troop.
Hingham Troop.
Holkham Troop.
Loddon Troop.
Norfolk Rangers.
Norwich Light Horse Volunteers.
Shropham and Guildcross Troop.
Tunstead and Happing Troop.
Yarmouth Troop.

*   *   *

Fig. 5: Shoulder-belt plate of the Walsham and Blofield Troop, *c.*1799.

The Peace was short lived and so most of the existing Troops renewed services in 1803. In November of that year Lord Townshend submitted a plan of forming the several Yeomanry corps of the County into regiments, a course calculated to add much to their efficiency, and this having received the approval of the Government, the following regiments were formed:

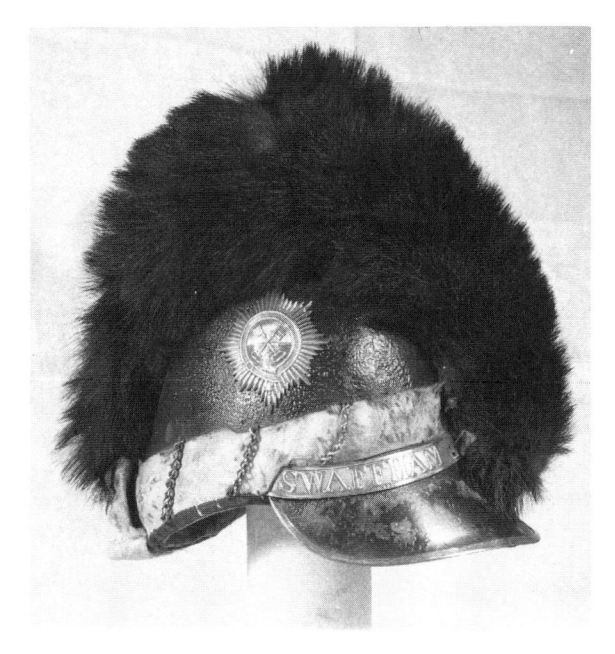

Fig. 6: Light Dragoon helmet of the Swaffham Troop. *c.*1800. Kind permission of Mr B. Mollo.

Amongst the tokens of a military nature issued between the years 1793 and 1797 is one minted for the Blofield Cavalry:– On the obverse: A mounted yeoman with drawn sword, 'Loyal Norfolk Yeomanry'; in the exergue, 'MDCCXCVI'. Reverse: a military trophy, 'Blofield Cavalry', 'Fear God and Honour the King.'

A fine shoulder-belt plate of the Walsham and Blofield Troop is also in existence (Fig. 5), a silver rectangular plate 2⁷/₁₀ths inches by 2 inches. The design consists of a large crown with the letters W and B at left and right respectively; below it the interwoven G R whilst below this the title NORFOLK at the foot. There is a quadruple scroll arranged in upward direction meeting above the crown, carrying the motto 'Teloque Animus Prestantior Omni'.

An actual Tarleton helmet of the Swaffham Yeomanry Cavalry is known, once in a private collection. The black leather helmet is in fine condition, has the usual fur crest and a white-out-of-red feather plume on the left side, a leopard-skin turban held in position by three small white metal

First Regiment.
Norfolk Rangers.
Lynn and Freebridge.
Holkham.
Smithdon and Brothercross.
Marshland.   Total strength 350.

Second Regiment.
East Dereham.
Swaffham.
South Urpingham.
South Greenhoe.
Hingham.
Wymondham.
Clackclose.   Total strength 408

Third Regiment
Norwich Light Horse.
Loddon and Clavering.
Tunstead and Happing.
Blofield and South Walsham.   Total strength 336.

It is interesting to find that, with few exceptions, most of the Troops forming the three Regiments were to survive for the next 25 year period, and that a certain number of portraits and paintings as well as a few actual uniform pieces are recorded.

In December 1795 a Standard was presented to the Clackclose Troop and mention is also made of a band of music belonging to this Troop being present. A shoulder-belt plate is known, oval, cast brass and with a shield in the centre carrying a castle with three turrets, (Norwich Castle), the title NORFOLK on a scroll above the shield and the words CLACKCLOSE and CAVALRY engraved left and right of shield respectively. A Standard of the Holkham Yeomanry Cavalry of 1798 carries the same central device, the three turreted castle on a shield with crown above and the letters H and Y left and right of shield and C below; a panel in each of the four corners. Fig. 3. The Standard of the Blofield and South Walsham Troop of 1795 also has the castle on a shield,[4] the Standard of Yarmouth Volunteer Cavalry. See Fig. 4.

Fig. 7: Lieutenant William Palgrave, Yarmouth Volunteer Cavalry, 1799. Reproduced from plate in Harvey's *Records*.

Fig. 8: Colonel John Harvey of Thorpe, Norwich, Colonel Commandant, East Norfolk Yeomanry Cavalry, but in the uniform of the Norwich Light Horse Volunteers, 1803. Reproduced from original portrait, colour plate in Harvey's *Records*.

shoulder-belt plate just visible below helmet lines which extend from back of collar to terminate at/or just below neck opening. Breeches are white. By 1806 the uniform is described as red faced black and it is likely to have been unchanged since the 1798/9 date[5]. (Fig. 7.)

The second painting shows Sir John Harvey of Thorpe, Norwich, a full length portrait standing with his charger; painting in St. Andrew's Hall, Norwich, Sir John having been Lord Mayor of that city in 1792. Uniform: (Norwich Light Horse Volunteers). Tarleton helmet with white over red plume and black turban. Scarlet jacket with gold lace, black collar edged gold with gold loop. Rounded black cuffs with flattened chevron in gold thereon. White breeches, black boots. White shoulder-belt with oval yellow metal plate with shield.[6] (Fig. 8.) (Colonel Harvey afterwards commanded the 3rd or East Regiment of Norfolk Yeomanry Cavalry from 1823-1828.)

The third painting is a watercolour now owned by the National Army Museum, believed to be by John Opie, who married a Norwich lady. The portrait is possibly that of a Mr. Carter of Norwich to whom a letter on the table is addressed, and in spite of a groom seen outside with horse, he is thought not to be an officer by reason of sword knot and cloth braid on collar, rather than gold or silver lace. The jacket is scarlet, buttons brass, collar and cuffs very dark blue or black, sword scabbard steel. (Fig. 9.)

* * *

chains crossing each side; on the right side of the helmet a white metal star badge, no inscription on garter surrounding the central device of crossed keys on crossed swords (Fig. 6). The remainder of the uniform would consist of scarlet jacket with blue collar and cuffs; two rows of silver braid all round collar and at tops of cuffs, showing scarlet light between. 20 loops of silver braid across chest, 7 inches long at top, 5 inches at bottom. Austrian knot on hip, and lace up side seam ending in crowsfoot. Double crowsfoot at bottom of the back. Jacket edged with white all round. Plated ball buttons in centre of front of jacket, half ball buttons on back of jacket.

The uniform period for 1799 to 1803 is covered by three known portraits showing dress of the Yarmouth Troop, Norwich Light Horse Volunteers and 3rd (or East) Regiment of Norfolk Yeomanry. The first of the trio shows Lieutenant William Pargrave, Yarmouth Troop, appointment dated 20 June 1798. His uniform is similar to that described for Sir Martin Folkes: – a Tarleton helmet, a long coat open from about the second or third button to display white waistcoat. He has a white kerchief, black stock and white shirt frill showing, six rows of (silver?) lace on chest, lace piping as coat edging, also on collar, cuffs and shoulder wings. White shoulder-belt with an oval(?)

Fig. 9: Portrait of a Yeoman of the Norwich Light Horse Volunteers, c.1800. Watercolour attributed to John Opie. Reproduced by kind permission of the National Army Museum.

Fig. 10: Diagram of a jacket of the Admiral Wodehouse Yeomanry. Reproduced from a Hawkes Tailors Book.

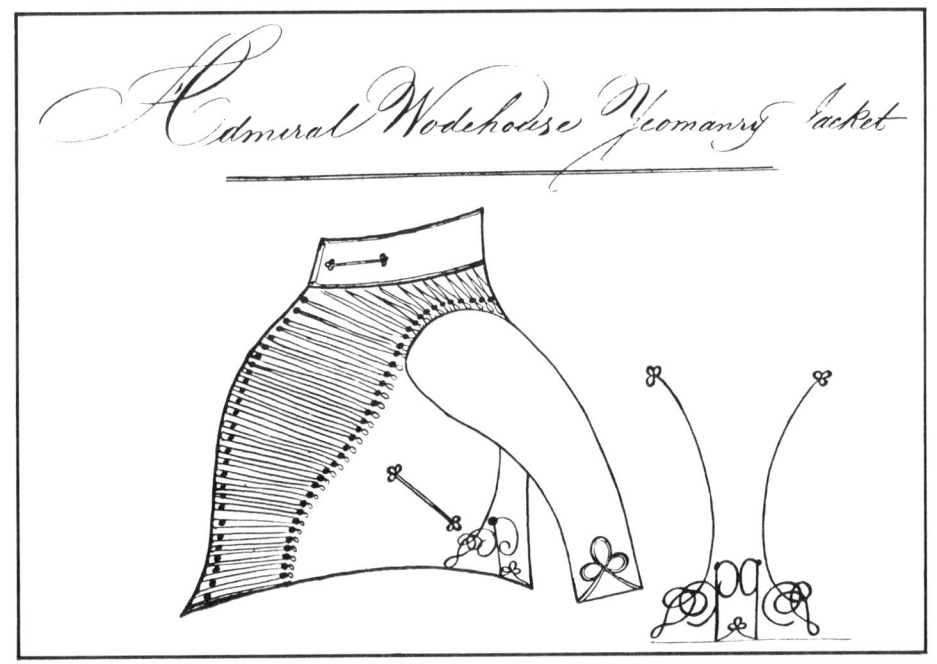

1806-1828

In 1806 James Willson compiled his 'View of the Volunteer Army of Great Britain', which was published 1 March 1807, being a comprehensive list of all Volunteer corps together with names of commanding officers and strengths of individual units; an accompanying 'schema' chart providing the colours of uniforms, facings, lace or braid, breeches or pantaloons, etc. The following is from that list and gives the mounted troops in Norfolk together with the various uniform colours then in wear:

	Jacket	Collar and Cuffs	Breeches	Lace
Blofield Cavalry	Red	Black	White	Gold
Clackclose Cavalry	Red	Blue	White	Gold
E. Dereham 1st Cavalry	Red	Black	White	Gold
E. Dereham 2nd Cavalry	Red	Black	White	Silver
Sth. Greenhoe Cavalry	Red	Black	White	Silver
Sth. Erpingham Cavalry	Red	Black	Blue	Silver
Hingham Cavalry	Red	Black	Blue	Silver
Loddon, etc. Cavalry	Red	Black	White	Gold
Marshland Cavalry	Red	Black	White	Silver
Norwich Cavalry	Red	Black	Blue	Gold
Norfolk Rangers	Green	Black	Green	Black
Smithdown, etc. Cavalry	Red	Black	White	Silver
Swaffham Cavalry	Red	Black	White	Silver
Tunstead, etc. Cavalry	Red	Black	Blue	Gold
Wymondham Cavalry	Red	Black	White	Gold
Yarmouth Cavalry	Red	Black	White	Gold
Lynn and Freebridge Legion Cavalry	Red	Yellow	White	Silver

Between the years 1806 and 1828 several Troops were raised but after comparatively short periods, disbanded, leaving little trace of their existence and still less of uniform. The following brief notes[8] give some details of the period but as far is is known no complete uniform or reliable portrait or painting has yet come to light.

1812. Norfolk Rangers, as before (1804), but the buttons now white metal, and Oxford grey overalls with silver stripe for officers, white for men. Officers now had silver pouch belts.

1815. Norfolk Rangers, dressed as in 1812 but the Waterloo Light Dragoon shako now in use; black plume (cock's feather for officers, horse-hair for the men).

1821. The First Regiment was reorganised, and the uniform was now very similar to the Rifle regiments of the time; the officers had silver epaulettes and a rather narrow silver stripe on their overalls.

1820-28. The dress pouch belonging to Colonel Harvey was made of a dark green or black material, edged silver lace and carrying the letters E N Y C on flap, a crown above and the figure 3 below.

1825. It is worth recording that about 1825 a Band was ordered for the 3rd or East Regiment, and that in 1827 copper kettle-drums were presented to the Regiment.

1828. On disbandment, the First Regiment wore a dark green double-breasted coatee with black velvet collar and cuffs braided with black and two rows of silver buttons; dark Oxford grey overalls with silver/white stripe; silver epaulettes for officers, plated shoulder scales for the men; Light Dragoon shako with black cock's feather plume for officers, black horse-hair for the men. Gold and crimson girdles for the officers, yellow and crimson for the men.

1820s. **The Admiral Wodehouse Yeomanry Cavalry.** The title and details of the jacket for this Troop are found in Hawkes Pattern Book. The garment is described as:– Scarlet superfine cloth jacket trimmed with silver Russian braid, black Genoa velvet collar and cuffs, the jacket edged round; plain Plated ½ ball buttons, lined with white shalloon, a silver loop on each shoulder. Fig. 10.

The title was probably one used locally as a friendly nickname for the Hingham Troop, 2nd or Midland Regiment, whose Commandant was Captain Hon. Philip Wodehouse, dated 28th September 1823. (Born in 1773 Philip Wodehouse entered the Royal Navy at an early age, was a Lieutenant by 1794, Captain R.N. 1797 and became Rear Admiral of the Blue 12 August 1819.)[9]

The Norfolk Fencible Cavalry, and the Provisional Cavalry of Norfolk.

Passing reference should be made to two bodies of cavalry bearing the county name: the Norfolk Fencible Cavalry and the Provisional Cavalry of Norfolk. Both had a comparatively short existence, the Fencibles from 1794-1800 and the Provisional Cavalry 1797-c.1800. Mention in Harvey's *Records* gives the following brief description of uniform common to both:– 'Uniform generally modelled on that of the Light Dragoons, namely, a furred helmet, short red or blue jacket, leather breeches or cloth pants, black gaiters or knee-boots with turned over tops. The Government in 1796 recommended the general adoption of this uniform for the Yeomanry and Provisional Cavalry, namely, a green jacket, with red facings and white lace, at 19s.; green cloth pantaloons at 10s.; leather cap and feather, 2s. 6d.; half boots 18s.; but it is needless to say that each unit adopted its own uniform according to the various tastes of their respective commanding officers.'

Hamilton Smith [7] provides details of the Norfolk Fencibles commanded by Lieutenant-Colonel Hon. William Assheton Harbord, the uniform as Light Dragoons, scarlet jacket with black facings, all lace silver, crested helmet with a white over red feather and a black turban. The first muster of the Norfolk Provisional Cavalry, Colonel William Earle Bulwer commanding, was ordered for 10 October 1797 in Surrey Street, Norwich. Records say that:– 'It is expected that each man appears on the day of muster cloathed with jacket, pantaloons, half-boots, hat and feather, agreeable to the pattern dress which may be seen at the house of Mr. Charles Reynolds, in the Market Place, Norwich; and that each man be mounted on an able mare or gelding, of the height of 14 hands or upwards, with the following horse furniture, (patterns of which may be seen at the house of Mr. John Frewer, in the Market Place, Norwich). A saddle with white cantle, bridle, breast plate and martingal, male pad and straps, cloak bag, holsters, collar with chain rein, horse rug and nose bag. N.B. The price of the cloathing £2.9s. – the horse furniture £5.'

Fig. 11: Front and side views of the 1831-42 helmet.

The Suffolk and Norfolk Border Yeomanry Cavalry, *c. 1833-c.1850*

We now turn to a controversial unit which included the county name Norfolk in its title. It is known to have existed between the years 1833-1850. There has previously been some misinformation about its uniform.

A veteran cavalry officer Sir Edward Kerrison, commanded the Suffolk Troop of a unit called the Suffolk and Norfolk Border Yeomanry Cavalry, Sir Edward being a Suffolk man who had recruited from the county border area and had accepted Norfolk men in its ranks. The strength of the Troop had probably dropped over the years and so it was ordered to be disbanded in March 1838. In the meantime however, around 1833, leading inhabitants of the border country held a meeting at Eye, Suffolk, with the object of forming a dining club, its raison d'etre, to give support and encouragement and to provide an annual dinner on the King's birthday, for members of the Troop. New rules and regulations were drawn up, members were elected by ballot and many influential people were enrolled, including two Lords, an

Admiral, an Archdeacon and many clergymen as well. The pay-list for 1833 records the names of George St.V. Wilson, Lieutenant and Officer Commanding, Sir Edward Kerrison as Captain; a Cornet, a Quartermaster, two Sergeants and two Corporals. It would seem therefore that although Sir Edward was still 'on paper' the Commandant of the Suffolk and Norfolk Border Y.C., the proposed new unit was to replace the old, hence Sir Edward's name appearing as a subordinate rank.

Sir Edward Kerrison, Bart., K.C.B., M.P., had entered the army in 1796 and ultimately reached the rank of General in 1851. He commanded the 7th Hussars from 1813-1815, serving at Orthes and Waterloo. A fine full length portrait at Oakley Park, Suffolk, was reproduced in full colour in Harvey's *Records,* and it is this painting which has misled artists about uniform.[10] The portrait shows him wearing a fancy uniform of a General Officer of Hussars, most probably one he designed for himself, consisting of tall Hussar busby with red bag and white plume, scarlet Hussar jacket, closely braided with gold chest lace, a pelisse of similar colour to the jacket, scarlet pantaloons with elaborate lace ornamentation to the thighs in conjunction with black Hessian boots with gold tassels. He wears the blue Sash and Badge of the G.C.H. and the Scarlet neck ribbon of the K.C.B., adding two brilliant colours, possibly mistaken by the artist as part uniform.

A painting, at one time in Holkham Hall, Norfolk, illustrates the uniform of a soldier of the Troop *c.*1830s, and is believed to be the only known evidence of dress:

Busby. Tall brown fur with yellow braid lines and scarlet bag. (No plume in wear).
Jacket. Scarlet, with dark blue collar and cuffs, close chest braid of yellow, apparently three rows of brass ball buttons. Yellow braid edging to collar and cuffs.
Pelisse. Blue. White fur around collar, around the bottom of garment and on cuffs. Again yellow braid covering the front either side of opening, with rows of buttons. Yellow braid design around cuff and two rows of ornamental braid on back of garment.
Overalls. Blue-grey with single broad scarlet stripe.
Shoulder-belt. White.
Sword-slings. White.
Sword scabbard. Steel.

The soldier in the painting is shown holding the reins of an officer's charger. It can be safely assumed that the officer's dress would be similar to that described above but with gold lace replacing the yellow braid, etc. The head-harness of the charger is shown decorated with cowrie shells, the saddle has a leopard skin cover, edged red, and the shabraque with pointed hind sections is dark blue with a broad scarlet inner border and gold lace outer border.

The uniform would have undergone some changes during the life of the troop, and is described by a former officer of the West India Regiment and later Uxbridge Yeomanry Cavalry, Burrows Wilcox Arthur Sleigh in April 1850 in his *The Royal Militia and Yeomanry Cavalry List.* The few facts given, albeit invaluable information, are recorded under Suffolk:—
Suffolk Borderers' Troop (Captain Commandant, Lieut.-General Sir Edward Kerrison, Bart.)
Regimental Appointments: 14th Light Dragoons; scarlet, with gold lace, chacos and plumes, swords and pistols.
Strength: Limited to 50 N.C.O.s and Privates. Band 6, in blue uniform.

* * *

1831-1849

Three Troops of the Norfolk Yeomanry Cavalry were raised in the Western part of the County:—

1st or Melton Troop.:— Captain Sir Jacob Astley, Bart.
2nd or West Rainham Troop.:— Captain Lord Charles Townshend.
3rd or Elmham Troop.:— Major the Hon. George John Milles.

The uniforms of these corps were mentioned in the *Norfolk Chronicle* of 24 September 1831 as consisting of red jacket, dark trousers and black helmets, the latter by no means of becoming shape. The grandson of the Marquis Townshend was largely responsible for the re-enlistment of many of the old Norfolk Rangers into the new Regiment. He went to London to choose and order the helmet which he did 'from the pattern of one I had seen in a French regiment during the Peninsula Campaign, with black horsehair depending over one side, the peak of black leather, edged with brass, fish scales for chains under the chin. The mountings of the officers helmets were gilt; the clothing of all was scarlet, with silver epaulettes, and brass scales for the officers and men; the trousers were blue, with red stripes, all cut in regular cavalry shape.' Fig. 11 gives two views of this helmet from which the following information can be gathered:— black japanned, gilt ornaments, lion's head ear pieces, with Gorgon pattern chin scales. Gilt crest. Black horsehair plume, 36 inches long, fitting over crest and hanging over the back. Helmet plate gilt raised 'W' on centre with 'A R' on either side. No crown.

The appearance and soldierly bearing of the Regiment may best be illustrated by an incident which occurred in 1835 during unrest amongst the farm labourers in the Docking area as described by Lieutenant Charles Loftus of the Rainham Troop:—

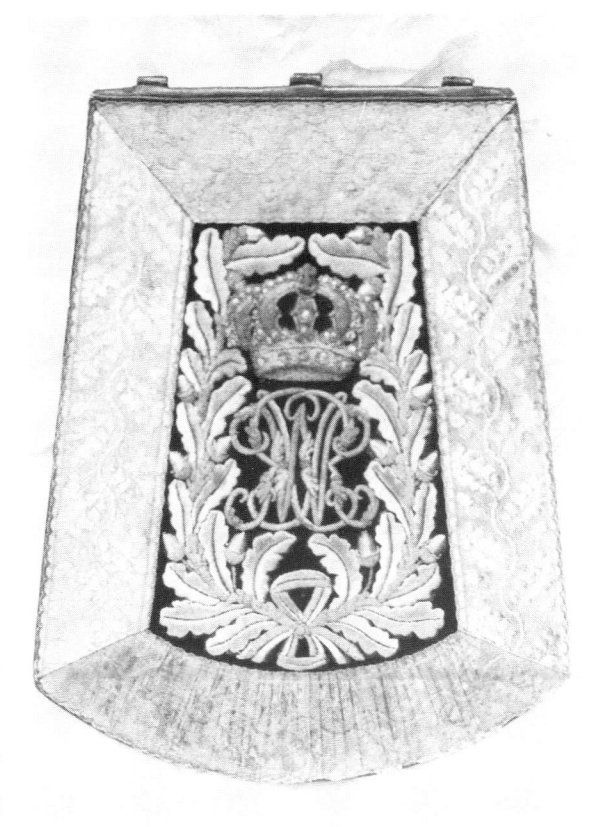

Fig. 12: Officer's dress sabretache, *c.*1831-37. Reproduced by kind permission of the Military Historical Society.

'Everything passed off quietly. The labourers who had created this disturbance were wonderfully surprised when they saw the soldiers coming, and so promptly, too, from far and wide (indeed we were much praised for our activity and zeal in assembling from all parts of the county on so short notice), and would not believe they were Yeomanry Cavalry, but the Dragoons from Norwich, our dress, as I have described, being that of heavy Dragoons, and completely deceived the locals.'

The heavy Dragoon uniform of the officers of the corps included a dress sabretache similar to the pattern used by officers of the regular regiments of Dragoons and Dragoon Guards. Fig. 12 shows a pattern believed to have been in use during the period 1831-37/38.

The Regimental Museum at Swaffham have in their fine collection dress items which belonged to a Captain P.R. Maillard, Adjutant from 1841-1844, his dress sabretache, waist-belt, pouch-belt and pouch. The sabretache is almost indentical to the earlier pattern but with VR cypher:– on red leather, silver stitching at top edge, scarlet cloth face, silver 1¾ ins. oak and acorn lace, double scallop. Silver wreath, silver VR, gold crown, silver jewels and pearls. The waist and swordbelt are on red morocco leather about 2 ins. width, silver oak and acorn lace. Dead gilt plate, carrying silver VR and crown, scrolls and wreath. The pouch-belt, about 2 ins. on red leather, two scallops to silver oak lace. No stripe. Pouch with scarlet cloth face, ¾ inch silver lace edging, silver buckle, tip and slide.

A forage cap (Fig. 13) belonged to a Cornet William Jex Blake of the Hingham Troop, 1843-6. It is of dark blue material, the top loose and not stiffened, made up in eight pieces with a basket button at centre, no lace figuring. There is a deep 2¼ ins. band of silver oak leaf lace and the black leather peak has silver braid edge, also a narrow black leather chin-strap.

Fig. 13: Forage cap of Cornet William Jex Blake, Hingham Troop, 1843-6.

In October 1838 the Hingham Troop was presented with a Standard by the Lord Lieutenant, Lord Wodehouse, and it is recorded that:– 'The Hingham Troop lately raised, was on this occasion assembled for the first time. The non commissioned officers and men have been selected with great care from the Yeomanry residing in the Forehoe Hundred, and the Troop has in its ranks some of the finest young men and best riders in the county, and all are well mounted on strong serviceable horses. The uniform is handsome, being like that of the 2nd Life Guards with silver instead of gold lace.'

In 1840 the Norfolk Yeomanry Cavalry is described as:– 'A fine body of men and with few exceptions, well mounted, there are indeed some superb horses amongst them. Their uniform and appointments (assimilating closely in cut and other details with those of Her Majesty's regiments of Dragoon Guards) contribute greatly to their soldierlike appearance. The full dress of the officers is very rich and becoming. Nor have we any hesitation in saying that the corps is one of which the county can justly be proud.'

Orders of dress from the *Regulations for Dress of the Norfolk Yeomanry Cavalry* were published in 1840:–

No. 1. Divine Service.
Officers; Scarlet Jacket and Epaulettes – Gold Girdle – Helmet – Silver Laced Overalls – Sword & Belt – Sabretache – Sword Knot – Gauntlets – Boots & Spurs and Foot Straps. The Orderly Officer with Pouch and Belt in addition. N.C.O.s and Privates: Scarlet Jacket with Shoulder Scales – Helmet – Overalls – Sword & Belt – Knot – Gauntlets – Boots (without Spurs) and Foot Straps.

No. 2. Under Arms, on Foot, for Inspections.
Officers: Blue Frock Coat with Scales – Trousers – Helmet – Sword & Belt – Undress Pouch & Belt – Sabretache – Knot – Gauntlets – Boots & Spurs and Foot Straps.
N.C.O.s and Privates: (As No. 1, but with trousers in place of overalls, and with pouch and pouch belt.)

No. 3. Sword Drill on Foot.
Officers: Blue Frock Coat with Scales – Overalls – Forage Cap – Sword & Belt – Sabretache – Knot – Boots & Spurs and Foot Straps – Gloves.
N.C.O.s and Privates: Undress Jacket – Trousers – Forage Cap – Sword & Belt – Knot – Shoes. Gloves and Foot Straps.

No. 4. Dismounted Guards.
The Orderly Officer will take charge of all Regimental Guards and will be dressed as for officers under arms on foot.
N.C.O.s and Privates: (As No. 1. with spurs.)

No. 5. Walking Dress and Cantonments.
Officers: Blue Frock Coat with Scales – Gold Girdle – Overalls – Forage Cap without case – Gloves – Boots & Spurs and Foot Straps.
N.C.O.s and Privates: Undress jacket – Forage Cap – Overalls – Gloves – Shoes or Boots & Foot Straps – Sword Belt.

No. 6. Marching Order.
Officers: Blue Frock Coat with Scales – Overalls – Helmet – Sword & Belt – Sabretache – Pouch & Belt – Knot – Gauntlets – Boots & Spurs and Foot Straps.
The Horse full accoutred, with Pistol, Cloak rolled and buckled on the holster, and black sheepskin over the saddle and valise.
N.C.O.s and Privates: Scarlet Jacket with Scales – Overalls – Helmet – Sword & Belt – Pouch & Belt – Knot – Gauntlets – Boots & Spurs and Foot Straps.
The Horse full accoutred, with Carbine & Pistol, the collar chain blackened and fastened round horse's neck, the Cloak neatly rolled 40 inches long and buckled over holsters. Stable Dress and Personal Necessaries in the saddle bags, which will be covered with the sheepskin and neatly buckled on the pad of the saddle behind.

No. 7. Review Order.
Officers: Scarlet Jacket with Epaulettes or Shoulder Scales (as may be ordered) – Gold Girdle – Cloth Trousers with Scarlet Stripes – Sword & Belt & Sabretache – Pouch & Belt – Knot – Gauntlets – Boots & Spurs and Foot Straps.
The Horse accoutred as in Marching Order, with the addition of the silver laced Shabraque under the Sheepskin, and no Valise.
N.C.O.s and Privates: The same as in Marching Order.

No. 8. Field Drill Order.
Officers: (as No. 3, but with trousers and gauntlets in place of overalls and gloves, and with the addition of the pouch and pouch belt.)
The Horse accoutred as for Marching Order.
N.C.O.s and Privates (As No. 6, but with scarlet jacket and scales and forage cap.)
(Horse furniture as No. 6, but no baggage, baggage straps or sheepskin).

No. 9. Watering Order.
Officers: (Dismounted, except the Orderly Officer, who will be mounted) (As No. 3, with gauntlets in place of gloves – shoulder scales are not mentioned.)
N.C.O.s and Privates: (As No. 3, without sword, sword belt or knot.)
The Regimental Saddle without Sheepskin, Cloak or Baggage: (with) Head Collar & Chain & Snaffle Bridle.

No. 10. Dinner Dress.
Officers: Scarlet Jacket and Epaulettes – Gold Girdle – Overalls with Silver Stripes – Boots with Plated Spurs and Foot Straps – the Orderly Officer with Pouch & Belt.
N.C.O.s and Privates: Undress Jackets – Trousers – Boots or Shoes (without Spurs) and Foot Straps.

No. 11. Court and Ball Dress.
Scarlet Jacket and Epaulettes – Gold Girdle (with Tassels) – Overalls with Silver Stripes – Sword – Dress Sabretache – Swordbelt and Sabretache – Sword Knot – Dress Pouch & Belt – Cocked Hat and Feathers – Gloves – Boots & Plated Spurs & Foot Straps.

No. 12. Attending the Inspection of Other Corps in the Field.
(As No. 7 – All Ranks.)

No. 13. Escorts (For Royal Family).
Should the Regiment be called upon to escort any of the Royal Family, the parties will at all times parade in Review Order.

No. 14. Escorts (For Prisoners).
Marching Order, unless otherwise ordered.

Notes: A black stock is ordered for all ranks in all orders of dress. The undress trousers appear to have been white.
The other ranks' 'undress jackets' were probably stable jackets.
A fine cocked hat belonging to a Cornet Denn Young of the Hingham Troop (Cornet 12 December 1838, Lieutenant in the Rainham Troop 25 March 1845 till 1849) as used for Court and Ball Dress, is in the Regimental Collection at Swaffham.

In 1842 Her Majesty was pleased to allow the Norfolk Yeomanry to be styled 'Prince Albert's Own Corps of Yeomanry Cavalry'. The helmets which previously bore a Maltese Cross, now had the Royal Arms, otherwise uniform was unchanged (Fig. 14). Items of the heavy cavalry uniform worn during the 1840s were described in a tailor's book of 1847:– 'Officer's coatee (probably Court or Levee dress). Scarlet with nine rows of silver lace as worn by the regular Dragoons unitl 1829. Two large silver loops on blue ground on either side of collar opening. Blue cuffs with (until 1847) three or four loops of silver lace (1847-49) a single loop of silver

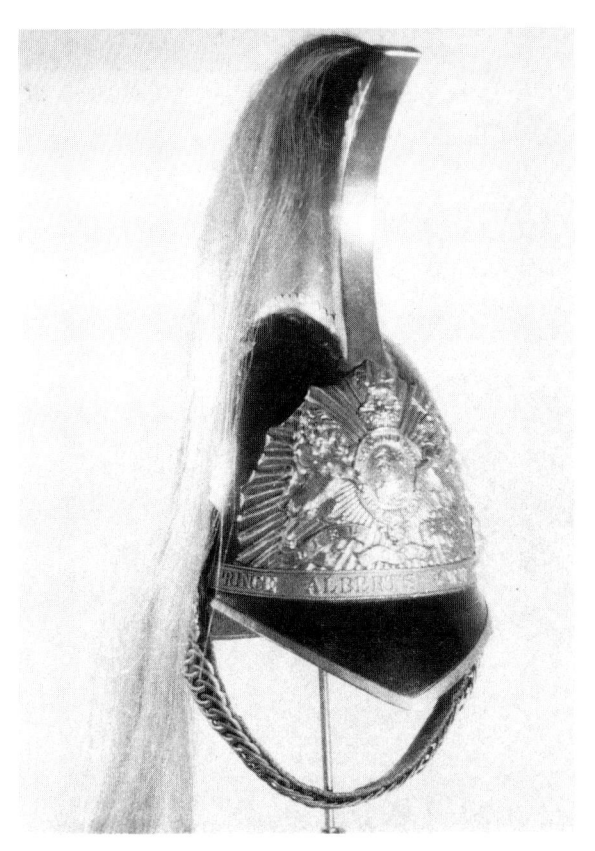

Fig. 14: Helmet, Prince Albert's Own Norfolk Cavalry, c.1843.

lace. Blue turnbacks on tail, fastened with a crown. Silver fringed epaulettes. Dress trousers blue with single broad silver stripe.
Undress Frock coat blue, single breasted, with nine white metal buttons down front and two on either side at back. White metal shoulder scales.'

1849. The Corps was disbanded ' in consequence of local circumstances' as it is quaintly noted in Harvey's *Records* and also in Jeremy Bastin's *The Norfolk Yeomanry in Peace and War 1782-1961* (1986).

Norfolk (Norwich) Mounted Rifle Volunteer Corps
1861-1862,
later **Norfolk (Norwich) Light Horse Volunteers**
1861-1867

Ten years after the disbandment of the Norfolk Yeomanry in 1849 the renewed threat of possible war with France led to the nationwide formation of the Volunteer Force – 1859/60. The city of Norwich was quick off the mark, setting up a Volunteer Rifle Corps that year, whilst later in 1860, at a meeting called for 23 December, it was proposed that a mounted corps of volunteer cavalry be founded. One of the original Rifle Volunteer officers, Mr. Francis Hay Gurney, a Norwich banker, who would have preferred a military career, offered to take the lead with its formation and undertook to obtain weapons, uniforms, drill books, etc. It was agreed that the new unit should be treated as mounted infantry rather than cavalry, although with 'a smart and rich dress, such as worn by the regular cavalry regiments and distinctive to that of Rifle Volunteers.' It was to be kept as a select unit of well trained mounted men with a minimum strength of 25, thus leaving scope for expansion, and that it was to be attached to the Rifle Volunteers for administration purposes. Although a Captain in the rifle volunteers, F. Hay Gurney took a step down to Lieutenant when appointed to command the new corps with effect 25 March 1861.

The uniform decided upon was described in Regimental Records:– 'The uniform consists of a scarlet tunic with blue facings, white cross belt, white breeches and Napoleon boots, the head dress is a busby with blue bag; the forage cap is blue trimmed with white. A number of Troop have daily appeared in the city during the week, on their way to drill; they are exceedingly well mounted and certainly present a very imposing appearance. The dress is decidedly gay and very conspicuous, just the reverse of that of the foot volunteers, whose quiet unobtrusive looking uniform will look still more modest (though we think not less effective) by the side of the Artillery blue and the mounted scarlet.' A review of the whole of the volunteers in the County took place on 12 September 1861 at Holkham Park and were inspected by Major-General Sir Archdale Wilson, Bart., K.C.B., and it is recorded that the Norwich Mounted Rifle Volunteers took part. Whether the headdress on that occasion was the Hussar busby is not certain, but by 1863 a helmet was worn.

In October 1862 this unit ceased to be a Mounted Rifle Volunteer Corps, and became a Light Horse Volunteer Corps with F. H. Gurney appointed Captain as from 13 October 1862.

Whilst there must be some doubt about the use of an Hussar busby, two dress items of the Light Horse are preserved at the Swaffham Museum, namely an officer's dress pouch and sabretache. The sabretache is of particular interest as it is the smallest specimen on record, the width of no more than 7 ins. at top and 8 ins. at bottom, overall depth 9 ins. There is a silver wave lace edging, about 1¼ins. wide, the face of ultramarine cloth, the design a crown, possibly of gold lace, a silver VR cypher below and a triple scroll below the cypher. The scroll is of scarlet cloth with silver lettering and edging and carrying the title:– NORFOLK LIGHT HORSE. Strangely enough the pouch is almost as broad as the top of the sabretache, the lace edging is silver but of a different pattern to the sabretache, the face is of ultramarine cloth with the interwoven letters N L H V below a crown, also in silver lace.

In 1862 the Norwich Light Horse participated in a Volunteer Fete held in September at Crown Point, whilst in March 1863 the city of Norwich celebrated the marriage of the Prince of Wales with a Grand Military Parade, 'The mounted Volunteers, who mustered very strongly on this occasion were conspicuous in their scarlet coats and showy helmets.' An illustration in the *Illustrated London News* of 26 September 1863 shows members of the Corps in Mounted Review Order at the annual review on Mousehold Heath (Fig. 15). At a similar review the following year at Gunton Park there is mention of performances given by the band of the 1st Norwich Light Horse.

Fig. 15: From the *Illustrated London News,* 26 September 1863. Review on Mousehold Heath. Norfolk Light Horse at left and right of picture.

In November 1866 the Prince and Princess of Wales visited Norwich, and the 1st Norwich Light Horse under Captain Hay Gurney had the honour of providing an escort for the royal carriage en route to Costessey Hall, the mansion of Lord Stafford. This duty no doubt gave the Light Horse a good feeling of 'one upmanship' as two Troops from the regular cavalry regiment at Norwich, the 1st King's Dragoon Guards, were delegated to street-lining duty shared with the Norwich Rifle Volunteers, the whole event duly recorded with a full page illustration in the *Illustrated London News* of 10 November 1866.

Additional pictorial evidence of dress comes from a painting showing Norwich Rifle Volunteer officers on the rifle range at Mousehold Heath during 1860s, two or three Light Horse officers in the midst, on this occasion in their Undress uniforms. This consisted of a blue kepi-shaped shako with silver braid band and piping, a scarlet stable jacket with blue collar and cuffs edged silver lace, blue overalls with double silver stripes.

To sum up therefore, the uniform of the Corps during its short existence was as follows:

Officers Full Dress: Blue cloth helmet with gilt mounts and red and white plume, with a triangle of leopardskin with an encrowned Royal Cypher in yellow metal. Scarlet Dragoon tunic with ultramarine collar and cuffs; silver cord all round collar, down front edge of tunic, on the back vents, on the pocket slits (trefoils at either end) and on the cuff according to rank (Austrian knot for subaltern officer, the same traced both sides with braid eyes for Captain); seven silver buttons down front, two at waist behind, silver cord shoulder straps. White breeches, black jack boots. Silver lace sword slings and pouch belt with dark (? blue) central line and gilt chains and pickers (Fig. 16).

Horse Furniture. Brown leather. Silver scales over forehead and silver lace brow band; silver bits, bosses and ear bosses. Black sheepskin edged red vandyke. No throat plume.

Other Ranks, Full Dress. Like the officers, but white in place of the silver, white trefoil on cuff. Silver chevrons for N.C.O.s. White pouch belt, no waist belt, black pouch, brown leather sword slings (Fig. 17). The trumpeter dressed like the men, but in reversed colours, i.e. bright ultramarine tunic with red collar and cuffs; trumpet slung on the back with bell on left shoulder, silver crossed trumpets on right sleeve above elbow.

It would appear from Figs. 15-17 that by *c.* 1863 blue overalls with double silver or white stripes had replaced the white breeches.

1867. The Corps disbanded. Subsequently a Norfolk Squadron was found for the Loyal Suffolk Hussars. Fig. 18 shows a portrait of Lieut.-Colonel F. Hay Gurney just prior to disbandment.

Fig. 16: Captain F. Hay Gurney, 1st Norwich Light Horse, 1861-67. Negative, kind permission by Mr D. W. Quarmby.

FOOTNOTES.

1. *Records of the Norfolk Yeomanry Cavalry.* From 1780-1908. Compiled by Lieut.-Colonel J. R. Harvey. Pub. Jarrold & Sons, London 1908.
2. Described in the *Index to British Military Costume Prints.* (Army Museums Ogilby Trust). No. 911.
3. Reproduced in colour in Harvey's *Records.*
4. Both reproduced in Harvey's *Records.*
5. Reproduced in Harvey's *Records.*
6. Reproduced in colour in Harvey's *Records.*
7. From Hamilton-Smith's Notebooks at the Victoria and Albert Museum.
8. Research by Lieut.-Commander Benson Freeman, O.B.E., R.N., Ret., and L. E. Buckell.
9. Marshall's *Royal Naval Biography,* Vol. I, Part II.
10. For example – The artist F. Stansell painted a large group consisting of 51 figures entitled 'Regiments of British Yeomanry. 1794-1914', which was published about 1914 as a large folding supplement plate for the *Boy's Own Paper,* this plate later reproduced in the *Tradition* magazine of the 1960s, No. 57, with notes about the numerous errors in the following No. 58. A figure appearing in this group was described as an officer of the Norfolk and Suffolk Borderers 1831, showing an all red Hussar uniform, obviously copied from the Kerrison portrait. (A rather fine original watercolour by the same artist, showing the same incorrect uniform, is in this author's own collection.)

The King's Own Royal Regiment.
The Norfolk Yeomanry.
1849-1900

With the disbanding of the Prince Albert's Own Yeomanry Cavalry in 1849, the County of Norfolk was effectively without a single corps of yeomanry, although the Norwich Mounted Rifle Volunteers, formed in 1861 and soon renamed 'The Norfolk Light Horse' filled the gap until 1867, when they too were disbanded. A period of some thirty years was to elapse before the County once again possessed its own corps of yeomanry. However, for some years prior to 1893, Norfolk men served as officers in the neighbouring Suffolk regiment of yeomanry cavalry. Furthermore, between 1893 and 1900 a complete troop composed of officers and men from Norfolk was maintained by the Duke of York's Own Loyal Suffolk Hussars. For this purpose, a troop sergeant major officially resident in Norwich was specially appointed to look after the interests of the Norfolk troop. There were also always a captain and a lieutenant who were resident in the County. Among the officers listed for the Loyal Suffolk Hussars in 1899 no less than eight were Norfolk men, including the Commanding Officer, Lieutenant-Colonel A. G. Lucas of Lowestoft.

* * *

During the South African War the Loyal Suffolk Hussars raised two companies for service in the conflict. They were the 43rd and 44th Companies of the 12th Battalion, Imperial Yeomanry, into which Norfolk men enlisted at Norwich in 1900, which subsequently served with distinction in the War.

1901-1914

Early in May 1901, while the war in South Africa was still in progress, His Majesty King Edward VII directed that a regiment of yeomanry should be raised in the County of Norfolk and caused the Lord Lieutenant, the Earl of Leicester, to send for Major H. A. Barclay. Major Barcley, who was then an officer in the Hampshire Carabiniers Imperial Yeomanry, was invited to undertake the raising and command of the new regiment, a task which he readily accepted. His Majesty further signified his wish that he should become Honorary Colonel, that the designation would be 'The King's Own' Norfolk Regiment of Imperial Yeomanry and that the Regiment should be armed and equipped as cavalry. The King also chose the uniform, which was blue with yellow facings and not the drab or khaki colour with which the yeomanry were currently being clothed. In addition, contrary to the regulations in force throughout the Imperial Yeomanry at this time, the other ranks of the King's Own were armed with swords and scabbards of the regular cavalry 1899 O.R.s pattern; they were also issued with Martini-Enfield cavalry carbines, *not* the long Lee Enfield rifles then in the process of being supplied to the rest of the Yeomanry Force. From the very earliest days of the Regiment the King took a great

Fig. 17: Sergeant, possibly Permanent Staff Instructor of 1st Norwich Light Horse, 1864. Central figure between Grenadier Guards Sergeant and 6th Dragoon Guards Sergeant at School of Musketry. Negative, kind permission R. J. Marrion.

personal interest in all matters pertaining to the King's Own, which was to continue until his death in 1910.

The County of Norfolk, with the royal residence and estate at Sandringham, presented a unique opportunity for the newly raised King's Own to carry out a wide range of ceremonial duties. Between 1901 and 1914, the corps was frequently to be called upon to perform mounted escorts, not only for the Royal Family but also for other royal visitors from Europe. Throughout this period, the Regiment also participated in many other important events and ceremonial occasions both within and outside the county.

The King was pleased to approve the formation 'of a Regiment of Imperial Yeomanry for the County of Norfolk to be designated the Norfolk (King's Own) Imperial Yeomanry' (*London Gazette* 24 May 1901 and A.O. 138/1901). Major Barclay was promoted Lt.-Col. and to command with effect 24 May 1901; and Captain J. H. Patterson, 20th Battalion, I.Y., was appointed the temporary Adjutant from 15 July 1901.

Fig. 19: Captain R. Harvey, D.S.O. commanding 43rd Company Imperial Yeomanry, in South Africa, 1900.

Fig. 18: Lieutenant Colonel F. Hay Gurney. Commanded 1862-67.

Recruiting was brisk. Colonel Barclay divided the county into convenient districts for his squadrons and allotted one or more local centres to each squadron, where the intending recruit could apply for full information regarding the Regiment. The following is an example of the announcements which appeared in the press at this period:

July 26th 1901   Imperial Yeomanry
King's Own Norfolk Regiment
RECRUITING

Gentlemen wishing to join the 'King's Own' are requested to submit their names or make personal application to any of the officers mentioned below.

A Squadron (Norwich and district with headquarters at Norwich) His Highness Major Prince Frederick Duleep Singh, Old Buckenham Hall, Attleborough; or Captain G. C. Buxton, Dunston Hall, Norwich; or to Second Lieutenant G. T. Bullard, Anchor Brewery, Norwich.

B Squadron (North-east Norfolk, with headquarters at North Walsham), Major J. R. Harvey, Holmwood, Thorpe, Norwich; or to Captain D. Spurrell, Bessingham Manor, Aldborough.

C Squadron (West Norfolk, with headquarters at Fakenham), Major C. D. Seymour, Barwick, King's Lynn; or to Captain A. Elwes, Congham House, King's Lynn.

D Squadron (South Norfolk, headquarters to be notified later) Major A. F. Morse, Earlham Lodge, Norwich.

Full particulars relating to the Regiment may be obtained at any time from the Adjutant, Hanworth Hall, Norfolk.

Gentlemen desirous of joining should make early application to one of the above centres.

In July-August of the same year a more detailed circular was issued by Colonel Barclay as follows:

IMPERIAL YEOMANRY
The King's Own Norfolk Regiment
Honorary Colonel – HIS MAJESTY THE KING.
Lieut.-Col. H. A. BARCLAY
HEADQUARTERS: 21 NORTHCOTE ROAD, MAGDALEN ROAD, NORWICH
ERPINGHAM GATE, NORWICH

Herein are set forth the Advantages, Pay, Duties and Compensations of this Regiment.

1. *Enrolment.* The term of service is for 3 years. Should a Yeoman be compelled to leave before the expiration of that time, the following scale of payments is enforced to assist in covering the loss to the Regiment.

   Under 1 year's service £5 0 0
   Under 2 years' service £3 0 0
   Under 3 years' service £2 0 0
   Over 3 years' service .... Nil

   No payment of any description is required on enrolment.

2. *Pay and Duties.* The following are the duties expected of a Yeoman each year, with pay where specified:–
   Recruits – 12 squad drills (before the training if possible).
   Trained Yeoman – 6 squad drills on foot and 3 mounted drills; also Annual Course of Musketry, for which pay is allowed at 3/-, and a maximum of 6/- per annum per man for Railway Expenses to the Range, for Annual Course of Musketry.

Permanent Duty. This takes place between 1st May and 30th September, at the time best suiting the Members of the Regiment, for 14 clear days.

3. *Horse at the Training* provided 'free' by Government, or £5 allowed to any man who brings a horse with him.

   Pay is at the rate of 5/6 per day, and 1/6 per day for forage for horse, for each Trooper. Non-Commissioned Officers, from 10/6 to 7/6 per day, with 1/6 per day added for forage.

4. *Compensations.* A sum not exceeding 3/6 per day may be granted for 6 months, in case of an injury to a Yeoman while on duty, and a sum not exceeding £30 for loss of a horse in the actual performance of duty.

5. *Expenses.* A smart Uniform, specially designed, and approved by His Majesty the King, consisting of Field Service Cap, Blue Serge Frock, Riding Breeches, Dress Frock with Yellow Facings*, Overalls*, and Helmet*, is provided *free* for each man. Brown Jack Boots are also provided.
   *These articles are not issued until a man has become proficient in putting his saddlery together and rolling his cloak properly.
   Arms and accoutrements, consisting of Sword, Short Rifle, Bandolier, Sword Belt, Sword Knot, Jack Spurs, Cloak and Haversack are supplied free.
   A complete set of Saddlery is provided for each horse, and is similar to that used in the regular Cavalry.

6. *Drills.* These will be held all over the County, in places most convenient to the members of the Regiment.

   Non-efficiency. A Yeoman who does not make himself efficient is required to make good the Government allowance thereby lost to the Regiment.
   In case of sickness preventing the performance of Permanent Duty and the necessary Drills, attendance at 3 Squad Drills and the Annual Course of Musketry will relieve a Yeoman from payment of the above, provided a Medical Certificate is sent to Headquarters before Permanent Duty.

   Musketry. According to existing regulations a Recruit has to fire his Recruit Course, 49 rounds, in addition to the Trained Yeoman's Course of 42 rounds for efficiency.

In District Orders dated 30 July 1901, sanction was given for Squadron Sergeant Major H. W. Pamplin (late 8th Royal Irish Hussars), permanent staff instructor of the Hampshire Imperial Yeomanry, to transfer to the Permanent Staff of the King's Own Norfolk Imperial Yeomanry as H.Q. Sergeant Major. (S.S.M. Pamplin later became Regimental Sergeant Major of the King's Own.)

The first assembly of the Regiment was held dismounted and in civilian clothing on the cricket ground at Holkham by permission of the Earl of Leicester; about 200 officers, N.C.O.s and men were present and the parade was inspected by Major General Lord Chesham, K.C.B., on 10 September 1901.

On 17 October 1901 the first official parade of the corps in public and wearing uniform took place at Norwich. In Regimental Orders dated 1 October the Commanding Officer expressed his wish 'that members would be on parade and also form a mounted Guard of Honour for the Countess of Leicester at a Grand Medal Presentation Parade at the Cavalry Barracks, Norwich, on the 17th October.' They were subsequently ordered to parade at 11 a.m. on the appointed day and further informed that uniform, arms and saddlery were to be issued early in October.

Fig. 20: The uniform as first approved by H.M. The King in 1901, showing the Other Ranks Mounted Review Order.

Those members of the Norfolk troop of the Loyal Suffolk Hussars with less that three years' service were now transferred to the new Regiment, while those with longer service had the option of transferring or remaining with their present regiment.

In November 1901, Captain Hon. J. Dawnay, D.S.O., 10th Royal Hussars, was selected for the adjutancy.

On 23 October 1901 an honour was conferred on the Regiment, when the following announcement appeared in the London Gazette of that date: 'Field-Marshal His Majesty The King to be Honorary Colonel of the Regiment'. This proved to be a powerful stimulus to recruiting, which from this date proceeded very briskly.

The next occasion when the services of the Norfolk Yeomen was required was when the King expressed a wish that the King's Own Norfolk Regiment of Yeomanry should find a mounted escort to Their Majesties the King and Queen, and Their Royal Highnesses the Duke and Duchess of

York, from Wolverton Station to Sandringham on 4 November 1901. This was to be the first of a very large number of Royal escorts and special duties to be carried out by the Regiment up to 1914. The Regimental Orders refer to this escort as follows: 'Saddlery and arms will be supplied as soon as possible to those members who have not already received them. Dress: helmet, spike and chain, dress frock, shoulder chains, bandoliers. N.B. (Officers, Sam Browne and sword), gauntlets, breeches, brown knee boots and spurs, saddlery complete, with the exception of rifle and bucket straps, which will *not* be worn. Sword frog on shoe case, sword with knot strapped to frog, cloaks on front arch.' About 200 members of the Regiment turned out on this occasion, under the command of Lieutenant-Colonel H. A. Barclay. Many of the men had been collected from the most distant ends of the County. They had come from Yarmouth, Stalham, North Walsham, Aylsham, Cromer, Holt, Norwich, Whitewell, Guestwick and Fakenham; the Midland and Great Northern Joint Railway ran special trains for their convenience from Norwich, Yarmouth and Cromer to Hillington where they detrained for a little preliminary drill in the park of Sir William ffolkes. From Hillington to Wolverton they travelled by road. The officers present were Colonel Barclay, Majors Prince F. Duleep Singh, J. R. Harvey, C. Seymour, A. Morse; Captains A. Elwes, G. Buxton; Lieutenants Collison, Spurrell, H. G. Barclay, Keppel, G. Gurney and Q. Gurney. By the King's special command, the Yeomanry were then ordered to parade in front of the hall, as this was the first occasion on which His Majesty had had the opportunity of inspecting the Regiment, which had been raised by his special desire, and he expressed approval of the way in which everything had been turned out at a few days' notice. His Majesty then commanded all the officers present at the escort to be presented to him, and at the same time invested Lieut.-Colonel Barclay with the Royal Victorian Order, Fourth Class, and expressed entire approval with the way in which the work had been carried out, and his pleasure at the great success attending the raising of the Regiment.

District Orders of 11th November announced that Captain Patterson was transferred to the Essex Imperial Yeomanry from 15 November 1901.

In January 1902 Colonel Barclay wrote to the officers as follows:

FROM THE OFFICER COMMANDING KING'S OWN NORFOLK IMPERIAL YEOMANRY TO THE OFFICERS K.O.N.I.Y.
NORWICH.   31st Jan. 1902

Sir,
It is His Majesty's wish that all officers of the Regiment should be presented at the forthcoming levee at St. James's Palace on Tuesday Feb. 11th next.

I have therefore to request that you will make arrangements to meet met at St. James's Palace at 12 noon on that day, at the entrance facing Marlborough House.
Dress to be worn:–
Full dress frock, medals and orders, overalls, wellington boots and steel spurs, helmet, spike and chain.
Sam Browne belt, sword and steel scabbard, white two-button kid gloves – plain backs.

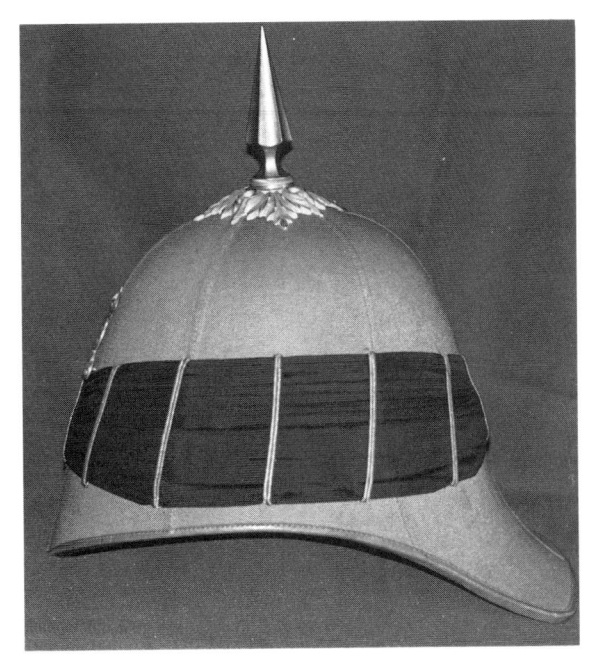

Fig. 21: Officers' Colonial Pattern Helmet 1901-1904. The cypher and crown badge is worn above the front of the pagri. ORs' helmets were basically the same, but with a plain drab pagri and plain brass spike. The spikes were replaced by drab buttons when not in review order.

Fig. 22: Dragoon Pattern Full Dress Helmet 1905-1914. Left, Officers. Right, OR's.

Cloaks will be worn to the Palace and left in the Hall and you will receive your orders there. Please acknowledge receipt of this letter per return of post to – The Adjutant, Yeomanry H.Q., Norwich.
Signed: – H. A. Barclay
Lieut. Col. Commanding K.O.N.I.Y

The officers present at the Levee were: Lt.-Col. H. A. Barclay, M.V.O., and Lt.-Col. G. F. Buxton, V.D.; Majors C. D. Seymour, H. H. Prince F. Duleep Singh, M.V.O., A. F. Morse, A. H. Elwes; Captains G. C. Buxton, A. R. Buxton, A. Collison, B. W. A. Keppel; Lieutenants E. D. Spurrell, W. L. Buxton, The Hon. C. S. M. Han-

Fig. 23: Officers' Dismounted Review Order, showing Colonel Barclay and his sons, from the left: 2nd Lieutenant H. G. Barclay, Colonel H. A. Barclay, M.V.O., 2nd Lieutenant J. F. Barclay. Note that only Colonel Barclay has six buttons fastening the full dress frock and that there are two braces on the Sam Browne, soon to be reduced to one.

bury, G. T. Bullard, Q. E. Gurney, G. R. Gurney, J. F. Barclay, H. G. Barclay, Rev. F. A. S. ffolkes, Surgeon-Captain J. F. Gordon-Dill, M.B., and Captain the Hon J. Dawnay (Adjutant).

Another honour was conferred on the Regiment when, in the *London Gazette* of 11 June 1902, it was announced that H.R.H. Prince Frederic Charles of Denmark was appointed to be Honorary Lieut.-Colonel in the Norfolk Imperial Yeomanry (King's Own).

On 3 June 1902 the Regiment mustered for the first time in Hillingdon Park. A spot in the Park within easy access of the railway station and village and within sight of the Hall, the residence of Sir William ffolkes, Bart., had been chosen as their camping ground. The four Squadrons covered the whole County. 'A' represented Norwich and district, 'B' East Norfolk, with North Walsham as a centre, 'C' South, Mid and North-West Norfolk, with Fakenham as its centre, and 'D' West Norfolk, with King's Lynn as its centre. Each Squadron was grouped together, both for men's quarters and stables, and the same division was maintained throughout at drills, at mess and in the tents.

During this training a contingent of 35 men under Major C. D. Seymour was sent to Aldershot to participate in the Grand Coronation Review there on Laffans Plain by His Majesty King Edward VII. The men wore their full dress of blue and yellow, with khaki helmets, and presented a smart and soldierly appearance. The King's Own Norfolks carried swords in place of carbines as a special distinction. A detachment consisting of one officer and nine O.R.s, mounted and in full dress, also represented the Regiment at the coronation of Their Majesties in London on 9 August 1902. For these services, Coronation Medals were awarded to Lieut.-Colonel H. A. Barclay, M.V.O., and Major C. D. Seymour.

Regimental Orders inform us that the corps was represented at a Garrison Church Parade also attended by the regimental band on 12 October 1902. The uniform for the occasion was dismounted Church Parade order, consisting of helmet with spike and chains, full dress frock, overalls, wellington boots and spurs, bandolier, sword with belts and knot and gauntlet gloves.

On November 15th the same year, the Norfolk Yeomanry were called upon to provide an escort from Wolferton Station to Sandringham on the occasion of a visit by His Imperial Majesty the Emperor of Germany to His Majesty King Edward VII. The Regiment provided a picked squadron of 13 officers and 157 men for this escort.

For the year 1903, it was decided to hold the second annual training at Skinner's Farm, near Cromer, on 28 May. As before, arrangements were made with the different railway companies to convey men, horses and baggage there. On behalf of the residents of Cromer, Major E. M. Hansell presented the Regiment with a challenge cup to be given to the best all round squadron as a memento of their encampment there. The Regiment was inspected by Sir William Gatacre, K.C.B.

In October 1903, the Regiment was again represented at the Garrison Church Parade in Norwich. The uniform prescribed was the same as for the previous year, but it was pointed out in orders that officers should have steel scabbards for their swords and that O.R.s would *not* wear bandoliers.

Towards the end of this year, a newly approved Levee tunic for officers and new gold laced pouch belt and pouch, sword slings and girdle were beginning to be worn at Levees and for balls.

A notice appearing in Regimental Orders of January 1904 reads: 'General Information to all Officers, N.C.O.s and Men. That F. A. Stone and Son of 11 Prince of Wales Rd., Norwich is appointed Regimental Tailor. In future all uniform will be supplied by them. Officers can obtain any articles of uniform sealed patterns as approved for the 'King's Own'. Prices on application.'

In the year 1904, the annual training was at Trowse, near Norwich, and on 3 August the same year, Captain J. F. Champion of the 14th King's Hussars was appointed Adjutant. A detachment of the King's Own under the command of Lieutenant G. T. Bullard took part in the ceremony at the unveiling of the Norfolk War Memorial at Norwich

Fig. 24: Review of the King's Own Royal Regiment by the Colonel-in-Chief, His Majesty King Edward VII and Honorary Colonel His Majesty King Haakon of Norway at Sandringham, 1 December 1906. (From a contemporary painting.)

on 17th October. The detachment consisted of 20 men, of which every man was in possession of a war medal. After the ceremony of unveiling, the trumpeters of the Regiment were selected to sound the 'Last Post'.

Northrepps Hall Park, near Cromer, was selected as the site for the annual training in 1905. The Regiment was inspected by General Lord Methuen, commanding the Eastern District, and Colonel T. O. W. Champion de Crespigny, Inspecting Officer of Imperial Yeomanry, who both expressed themselves as absolutely satisfied with the efficient state of the Regiment.

On 5 October 1905 a mounted escort and dismounted detachment from the Regiment, under Lieutenant G. T. Bullard, together with the band of the Regiment was present at the laying of the foundation stone of the New Cavalry Barracks at Norwich by the Secretary of State for War, Mr. Arnold Foster. The Regiment also provided an escort for Her Majesty the Queen and His Majesty the King of the Hellenes at Sandringham on 24 November 1905.

On the accession of Prince Charles of Denmark to the Kingdom of Norway, – he assumed the title of King Haakon VII – the commanding officer wired the congratulations of the officers, N.C.O.s and men of the Regiment to His Majesty the King of Norway on his entering his kingdom on 25 November 1905. In the *London Gazette* of 22 December the following announcement appeared:

'His Majesty the King has been graciously pleased to approve of the Norfolk (King's Own) Imperial Yeomanry being in future designated The King's Own Royal Regiment, Norfolk Imperial Yeomanry.

The King has graciously pleased to confer upon the King's Own Royal Regiment, Norfolk Imperial Yeomanry, the honour of becoming its Colonel-in-Chief; (he had formerly been Honorary Colonel.)

Imperial Yeomanry, The King's Own Royal Regiment, Norfolk Imperial Yeomanry, His Majesty King Haakon VII of Norway, G.C.B., G.C.V.O., from Honorary Lieut-Colonel to be Honorary Colonel, dated 23rd December.'

It was probably as a compliment to King Haakon that, earlier in the year, a new full dress helmet which was of slightly Germanic appearance had been adopted (see Uniform Details below for description).

East Dereham was approved as a drill station for 'C' Squadron in 1905.

The following extract from Regimental Orders issued early in 1905 is of interest, particularly in respect of the rare instructions concerning the 'Patterson' equipment for carrying the rifle. Captain J. H. Patterson, who invented the system, had served as temporary Adjutant of the King's Own from 15 July 1901 until his transfer to the Essex Imperial Yeomanry on 4 December the same year. The Essex, like the Norfolk Imperial Yeomanry, were to use this method of carrying the rifle, but only for a short period.

Regimental Orders 1905.

Change of Uniform. In continuation of Regimental Order No. 5 of October 1904, it is notified for General Information that a New Helmet for the Regiment has been approved by His Majesty and will shortly be issued, also Blue Pantaloons with Dragoons's Yellow stripes.

Magazine Lee-Enfield Rifles. (a) These rifles have been issued to the Regiment in place of the Martini-Enfield Carbines recently called in.

(b) Men will be drilled with the new rifle as often as possible, and taught the Manual Exercise.

They must also be made thoroughly acquainted with 'the action' and names and parts of the rifle.

(c) The bolts of rifles are not to be changed, for an interchange may seriously affect the shooting of a rifle.

The number on the bolt should correspond with the number on the body of the rifle just in front of the bolt head.

P.S.S. (Permanent Staff Sergeant) Majors will keep a record of the number of the bolt of each rifle in their Equipment Issue Ledger (opposite the number of the stand of arms as shewn on the butt plate).

Shooting Competitions. The Commanding Officer hopes that now the Regiment is armed with the rifle, the greater interest will be taken in the various Shooting Competitions during the summer.

All particulars can be obtained from the Orderly Room, and Officers Commanding Squadrons will render a list of any men wishing to compete.

The Patterson Equipment for Carrying the Rifle Mounted or Dismounted. This will be issued to every Non-Commissioned Officer and Man immediately on receipt by Squadron:–

Fig. 25: Badges and buttons. It will be apparent that this Regiment, wearing the Royal Cypher as a badge, on the accession of King George V in 1910, there was in consequence a change of that badge. This is clear in the badges shown here. Helmet plates, pouch badges, chevrons and proficiency badges are described in the main text.

On the colonial *helmet* 1901-05 No. 1 was worn in gilt by officers, and in gilding metal by other ranks. On the *forage cap* other ranks wore in gilding metal No. 1 1902-10 and then No. 9 1910-14. Officers wore a crowned EviiR cypher in gold embroidery on dark blue of similar height to No. 8 1902-10, and then No. 8 1910-14 when King George had acceded.

On the *field service cap* officers wore a gold on dark blue crowned EviiR cypher of similar size to No. 2 1901-02 only. Other ranks wore no badge on the *field service cap* until its reintroduction in the 1930s (when No. 8 was worn).

Officers wore a silver badge similar to No. 2 until 1910 and then No. 9 in silver 1910-14 on the collar of *mess dress* and *levee dress*; whilst on their *mess dress* other ranks wore No. 2 in gilding metal 1902-10 and then No. 4 1910-14.

On the *collar* of the blue frock other ranks wore in gilding metal: a royal arms similar to No. 3, but without the scroll, 1901-02; a badge similar to No. 3, but only 31×29mm, 1902-05; and No. 4 1906-14.

On the frock *shoulder chains* officers wore No. 1 1901-10 and then No. 8 1910-14, both in gilt; while other ranks wore No. 1 1901-10 and a badge similar to No. 8, but 50×43mm, 1910-14. From 1906 to 1914 all ranks wore No. 7 on the *shoulder chains* below the crowned cyphers.

On the *collar* of the frockcoat worn by officers and the bandmaster 1906-14 a gilt badge, similar to No. 2, was worn until 1910 and then No. 10 in gilt 1910-14.

On the *service dress* officers wore No. 8 on the *cap* and No. 4 on the *collar*, both in gilt; while other ranks wore No. 8 on the *cap* and a *shoulder title* similar to No. 7, but only 43×13mm, both in gilding metal, but no collar badges.

No. 6 is the officers' silver *pouchbelt plate* worn 1903-10. In 1910 the cypher was changed to GvR but the scrolls were not altered.

Senior NCOs wore gilding metal *badges* above their *chevrons* as follows:
(A) On frocks: 1901-02 royal arms as No. 3 but without the scroll; 1902-05 No. 3; and 1906-14 similar to No. 4 but 51×46mm.
(B) On mess dress: 1901-02 as on frock; 1902-05 as on collar of the frock: and 1906-14 No. 4.

Buttons, in gilt for officers and in gilding metal for other ranks were No. 5 1902-10 and then No. 11 1910-14, except that other ranks wore royal arms buttons in service dress.

K. Hook Collection

The Equipment consists of:–
"BELT FROG" and "SADDLE FROG"
The 'Belt Frog' consists of a loop and short sling strap (with hook) all in one piece. The Frog is worn on the belt behind the left hip.

The 'Saddle Frog' consists of a flat piece of leather to which a moveable steel grip, to take the small of the butt, is firmly fixed by means of a steel rivet and pin. A strap fastens the Frog to the near side of the saddle so that it rests against the round part of the horse's side and fairly close to the flap of the saddle. It is kept in this position by means of the Frog arm which is secured to the girth or girth straps.

Directions. To attach the rifle to the Belt Frog, pull the loop into sight with the left hand and pass the muzzle of the rifle through it, holding the rifle with the right hand at the point of balance, then drop the left hand on to the hook on the sling strap and fasten it to the trigger guard. The rifle or carbine is then securely attached to the man.

To Mount: Mount in the ordinary way as if no rifle were carried. When mounted seize the rifle below the breech with left hand, turn it very slightly inwards and press the small of the butt smartly into the grip. The sling strap should be quite loose when the rider is mounted, so that when he rises in the saddle there will be no pull on the rifle.

To Dismount: Dismount as if without arms, as the motion of the body in dismounting disengages the rifle from the 'Saddle Frog', To disengage the rifle from the Belt Frog, release the hook from the trigger guard and slip the muzzle of the rifle out of the loop.

To Disengage the Rifle when Mounted: 1st. Release the hook from the trigger guard. This is easily done by twisting the rifle round in the clip so that the trigger guard stands out.
2nd. Release the rifle from the Saddle Frog by seizing it above the back sight, twisting it to the left, and at the same time giving it a strong outward pull, then slip the rifle out of the loop and pass it to the right hand under the reins.

Only twelve months later, in an extract from Regimental Orders dated March April 1906, inform us that 'In view of the fact that a considerable number of rifles have been damaged by the Patterson Clip Equipment, the Commanding Officer has decided to equip the Regiment with the Service Rifle Bucket Mark III instead of the Patterson Clip. All Patterson Clips should be returned to store immediately.'

In May 1906 new drill stations at Fransham, Watton and Wells were fixed for 'C' Squadron and those at Wramplingham, Hillington, Rougham and Burnham Market were closed. Annual training this year was carried out at Hunstanton and at the end of June the strength of the Regiment was:

Squadron	Officers	Others	Total
A	12	100	112
B	5	93	98
C	4	92	96
D	4	95	99
Total	25	380	405

A valuable and comprehensive list of all the clothing, arms and accoutrements of the Other Ranks is to be found among the Regimental Orders. It provides an unrivalled insight into the cost of these items for an Imperial Yeomanry Regiment of this period and for that reason is presented in full.

Fig. 26: Front view, Officer's Levee Tunic 1903-1914, collar and cuffs laced for a field officer.

Fig. 27: Rear view, Officer's Levee Tunic 1903-1914.

Regimental Orders 1906			
Price List of Clothing in 1906	£.	S.	D.
Dress Frock, lined	0.	16.	6
Shoulder Chains, pairs		3.	6
Shoulder Cyphers, pairs		2.	0
Shoulder Letters, pairs (K.O.R.R.)		1.	0
Collar Badges		1.	0
Undress Frock, Unlined		12.	6
Breeches	1.	2.	6
Overalls, with yellow stripe		17.	6
Fatigue overalls		6.	0
Helmet, with furniture	1.	0.	0
Helmet Spike and chain sets		4.	0
Helmet Plume		4.	0
Helmet Plume Case			6
Helmet Bag		1.	0
Cloak	1.	10.	0
Cloak Belt		2.	6
Gauntlets, pairs		6.	0
Jack boots, pairs	1.	5.	0
Jack Spurs, and Straps and Shields		4.	0
Spurs, Swan Neck, pairs		2.	6
Putties, pairs, 1st quality		3.	6
Putties, pairs, 2nd quality		1.	6
Forage Cap and Badge (N. C. Officers)		12.	6
Forage Cap and Badge (Troopers)		5.	6
Sergeant's Chevrons, Worsted and Cloth, set of three		1.	6
Sergeant's Chevrons, Gold Lace, set of three		9.	0
Corporal's Chevrons, Worsted and Cloth, set of two		1.	0
Corporal's Chevrons, Gold Lace, set of two		6.	6
Crowns for Sergt. Majors' Worsted		1.	0
Crowns for Sergt. Majors' Gold Lace		3.	6
Gold Lacing Sergt. Majors' or Sergts.' D. or U. Frock		4.	6
N.C.O.'s Arm Badges		1.	6
Trumpeters' Badges, Worsted		1.	2
Trumpeter's Badges, Gold		3.	0
Shoeing Smith's Badges, Worsted		1.	2
Shoeing Smith's Badges, Gold		3.	0
Saddlers' Badges, Worsted		1.	2
Saddlers' Badges, Gold		2.	6
Signallers' Badges, Worsted		1.	6
Signallers' Badges, Gold		3.	6
Best Shot, Sergts. and Lance Sergts.' Badges, Gold Lace		7.	6
Best Shot, Sergts. and Lance Sergts.' Worsted		2.	6
Best Shot Corpl. and Troopers Badges, Gold Lace		7.	6
Best Shot Corpl. and Troopers Badges, Worsted		2.	6
Best Shot in Squadron, Cross Guns and Star, Gold Lace		3.	6
Best Shot in Squadron, Cross Guns and Star, Worsted		1.	0
Marksman's Badge, Gold Lace		2.	6
Marksman's Badge, Worsted		1.	0
Scouts' Badges, Regimental		1.	0
Scouts' Badges, Squadron			9
Arms			
Rifle, M.L.E. (magazine Lee Enfield)	3.	10.	6
Sliding Bar Backsight		1.	6
Protectors, Foresight			6
Pull-throughs, complete			6
Pull-through cord and gauze only			3
Reflector's Mirror		1.	9
Morris Tube – .303		17.	6
Swords, pattern 1899	1.	2.	0
Swords, Scabbards 1899		9.	0
Belts, Waist – Brown Leather		3.	5
Billets, Swords, pairs, leather		1.	6
Knots, sword			9
Bandoliers		10.	6
Bugles		12.	3
Trumpets		9.	0
Strings for both, each		1.	0
Patterson Rifle-Carrying Equipment, complete	1.	0.	0
Patterson Waist Belt only		5.	0
Patterson Shoulder Strap		3.	0
Patterson Rifle Loop		4.	0
Patterson Sword Slings, pair		4.	0
Oil bottle for rifle			6
Sliding Bar, Backsight cover		1.	6
Saddlery			
Ropes, Head, Hemp		1.	0

Bridoons		8
Bits, Portsmouth, with Head Stall and Reins	8.	0
Blankets	6.	6
Breastplates and Top Straps	5.	0
Head Collars, complete	6.	6
Frogs, Sword	3.	0
Girths	4.	0
Stirrup Irons, pair	3.	0
Stirrup Leathers, pairs	5.	0
Numnahs	6.	9
Brass Runners, pairs		3
Bridoon Reins	3.	6
Saddles	2. 10	0
Cloak and Wallet Straps, pairs	3.	0
Shoe-case Straps		6
Baggage Straps (set of three)	2.	0
Centre Cloak Straps		9
Surcingle	5.	0
Wallets	14.	0
Shoe Cases	3.	0
Ropes, Head, White Cotton	1.	3
Rifle Bucket for Saddle	10.	6
Rifle Bucket for Cycle	17.	6
Flag Bucket for Saddle	12.6	

Fig. 28: Officer's Levee Order 1905. It depicts the 7th Marquess Townshend, born 1916, when he was a Second Lieutenant, at a Levee in 1938.

The regiment was once again called on to provide an escort for the King and Queen when they opened the new King Edward VII Grammar School at King's Lynn. Their Majesties expressed their pleasure at, and approval of, the escort and especially remarked on the smartness of the turn-out and the good quality of the horses. Major A. H. S. Elwes was invested with the Royal Victorian Order, Fourth Class, on this occasion (*London Gazette* 9 November 1906). On 23 November 1906, the Regiment was again ordered to provide an escort under the command of Major C. D. Seymour, for Their Majesties the Queen and King Haakon VII and Queen Maud of Norway at Wolferton, on their return to their Norfolk residence. King Haakon conferred the Order of St. Olaf on Major Seymour.

On 1 December, by His Majesty's command, the Regiment paraded in review order, mounted, for the purpose of being inspected by their Colonel-in-Chief, His Majesty the King, and their Honorary Colonel, King Haakon. The Regiment marched past at the walk, trot and gallop before the two sovereigns, who commanded Colonel H. A. Barclay, M.V.O., the commanding officer, to convey to all ranks their Majesties' very great

Fig. 29: Officer's Full Dress Pouch 1903-1914. This particular example dates from the period 1901-1911, although it may well have been worn later.

satisfaction at the way the Regiment turned out for the royal review at Sandringham. On this occasion, King Haakon conferred the Insignia of Commander of the Order of St. Olaf on Lt.-Colonel H. A. Barclay, M.V.O. The Adjutant of the Regiment, Captain John Francis Champion, 14th King's Hussars, was appointed a Member of the Royal Victorian Order, Fourth Class, and the King was also graciously pleased to promote Colonel Henry Albert Barclay, M.V.O., to be a Commander in the Royal Victorian Order.

In 1907 the annual training of the Regiment took place at Sheringham from 29 May to 13 June. The Regiment was again inspected by General Lord Methuen, who was delighted with what he saw, and the great keenness and intelligence shown by all, and was much struck with the knowledge which all ranks had of their duties. This report was submitted by Lord Methuen to the King.

On 4 November 1907 by command of The King, the King's Own was called upon to provide an escort for Their Majesties the King and Queen of Spain at Wolferton when they visited The King at Sandringham. The numbers that attended were 11 officers and 121 rank and file. On the 9th of the same month, The King was graciously pleased to approve of Lt.-Colonel H. A. Barclay, C.V.O., commanding the Regiment, being appointed aide-de-camp to His Majesty and to confer upon him the rank of Colonel in the Imperial Yeomanry.

In 1908 the King's Own Royal Regiment became part of the new Territorial Force, brigaded together with the Loyal Suffolk Hussars and the Essex Yeomanry as the Eastern Mounted Brigade. This year the annual camp was again held at Sheringham. On 3 August 1909 Captain the Hon. R. N. D. Ryder, 8th Royal Irish Hussars, was appointed adjutant.

Fig. 30: Troop in Drill Order, 1905. All wear the blue drill or field dress with the blue pantaloons and puttees introduced in 1905. Note the short lived Patterson clip method of carrying the rifle.

The annual training was carried out at Cromer and, on October 25th, in an impressive ceremony, The King presented a guidon to the Regiment, which paraded in mounted and dismounted review order.

In London on 10 May 1910, a mounted detachment in review order, composed of one officer and 24 O.R.s, performed the sad duty of riding in the funeral procession of their Colonel-in-Chief, King Edward VII. The party rode near the head of the procession with detachments from the Duke of Lancaster's Own and the Queen's Own Oxfordshire

Fig. 31: The Officers in Dismounted Review Order c.1905. This photograph was probably taken at the Annual Camp of 1905. It shows the dismounted review order as worn from 1901, but with the 1905 pattern black helmets and yellow plumes. Further changes occurred in 1909, when the Sam Browne belt was replaced by the gold laced pouch belt and sword slings and short white gloves were substituted for the brown leather gauntlets. Colonel Barclay (seated 5th from right) remains the only officer with a six-button fastening to his full dress frock. The Adjutant, Captain J. F. Champion of the 14th King's Hussars, is seated 2nd from right, and on Colonel Barclay's left is Major and Hon. Lt.-Col. G. F. Buxton, V.D.

Hussars, of which The King had also been Colonel-in-Chief. The annual camp took place from 20 July to 6 August at Crown Point, Norwich.

In 1911 a detachment of one officer (Captain G. T. Bullard) and 25 O.R.s represented the King's Own Royal Regiment at the coronation of King George V, when they paraded in London dismounted, in review order, on 22nd and 23rd June to carry out street lining duties. In July, a mounted escort was furnished for His Majesty's visit to Norwich on the 8th of that month. It is worth noting that by this year, in a period of only ten years, the King's Own Royal Regiment had particpated in about 14 escorts as well as reviews and other important ceremonial occasions, which is probably a record for a yeomanry regiment.

Northrepps Hall Park, near Cromer, was chosen for the annual camp in 1912, and in 1913 it was held at Beccles in Suffolk.

On 6 September 1913, Colonel H. A. Barclay, C.V.O., T.D., A.D.C., retired from the command and was succeeded by Lieut.-Colonel C.D. Seymour; both these were later (*L.G.* 7 October 1913) ante dated to 24 May 1913. On 1 November that year Captain G. T. McMurrough-Kavanagh, 7th Queen's Own Hussars, was appointed adjutant.

In 1914, the Regimental Headquarters was listed as Cattle Market Street, Norwich, and the last annual camp prior to the First World War was held at Holkham Park.

Uniform – General Notes
1901-1914

On the formation of the Regiment in 1901 the headdress adopted for Full and Field dress was a drab Colonial pattern helmet fitted with a detachable spike and mount. There was no Full Dress tunic in the proper sense of the word for either officers or men. In its place a dark blue serge frock or patrol jacket was selected for all duties; khaki uniform was not taken into service at this time. The reason this particular type of uniform came to be chosen can be found in information contained in a letter preserved in the Regimental Collection, dated 5 June 1901, which was written by the newly appointed commanding officer, Lt.-Colonel H. A. Barclay, to his wife immediately after an audience with The King in which the subject of uniform was raised. Colonel Barclay had proposed a form of khaki, a suggestion to which His Majesty replied, 'No, none of that convict stuff for my regiment.' The King then promptly sent for a set of his own blue patrols, which in this instance were probably those of a General Officer, as an example. Certainly, the pattern chosen by the King's Own was very similar to that described in the 1900 Dress Regulations for General Officers but with the addition of yellow facings and shoulder chains. Colonel Barclay also requested that His Majesty might consent to the use of his A.D.C. badge and buttons, both of which showed the Royal Cypher, a request to which His Majesty was pleased to agree.

Fig. 32: Officer's Forage Cap, 1902-1914. This staff pattern cap, adopted by the officers in 1902, shows the staff style of leaf embroidery as worn by Colonel Barclay.

Fig. 33: Officer's Forage Cap 1902-1914. As Fig. 32, but with the plain peak of officers below field rank.

Fig. 34: Field Service Cap, 1901. Although this cap may have been made in the 1930s, it is basically of the same pattern as that first worn in 1901 and, informally, much later by some officers.

The uniform first approved by The King for the other ranks can be seen in a fine portrait photograph, now in the Regimental Collection, taken in early 1901 (Fig. 20). In the event, a small embellishment in the form of a yellow cord edging to the cuffs forming a trefoil over the point was not adopted, nor were the straight cut breast pocket flaps, which were changed for ones of triangular shape. The type of bandolier shown in the photograph was not, for some reason, taken into service. Instead, bandoliers of the *c.*1881 Mounted Infantry pattern were issued.

When the Full Dress version of the frock or jacket

appeared, there were yellow gorget patches on the collar and the pointed cuffs were faced yellow. The officers were distinguished by rows of gold braid over the cuffs and all ranks frocks were fitted with shoulder chains for both Full and Undress wear. However, the Undress garments, while retaining the yellow gorget patches, had plain blue cuffs. The officers' sleeves had the same gold rank markings as on the Full Dress frock (see Fig. 35).

For mounted duties, all ranks wore drab cord riding pantaloons with narrow yellow piping in the side seams and their brown knee boots, which had 'V' cuts at the top in front, were worn with jack spurs. When employed dismounted, officers and men wore blue overall trousers with broad 1¾ inch yellow cloth side stripes, strapped over black Wellington boots and box spurs.

At first the officers had Sam Browne belts fitted with *two* shoulder braces (Fig. 23). This arrangement was shortlived however, and a single brace carried over the right shoulder was adopted. For Full Dress occasions, the officers' swords had gold knots and the scabbards ordered were of steel, while for Undress and Field duties leather-covered scabbards with leather knots were regulation. It is known that the swords and scabbards issued to the other ranks from formation were of the regular cavalry 1899 pattern with a brown leather knot but the precise pattern of sword used by the officers has not been established definitely, although photographs suggest that it was very similar to the 1896 regular cavalry officers pattern with a bowl guard of pierced design. In a list of various items supplied by the Regimental Tailors to 2nd Lieutenant Ivor Buxton, dated 31 January 1906 is shown a sword with gold knot and steel scabbard, the sword to have the 'regimental crest and motto', this was probably featured on the hilt or guard of all officers swords. Between 1901 and 1908 (except, from 1903, when in Levee Order) officers on dismounted duties carried the sword on the Sam Browne belt. For the other ranks, it was carried by means of brown leather slings from a waist belt worn under the serge frock, a method which continued until 1904. For all mounted duties both the officers and men carried their swords in a frog attached to the shoe case suspended from the nearside of the saddle. Exceptionally, one or two photographs show mounted officers retaining the sword on the Sam Browne.

The bandoliers adopted in 1901 appear to have been used by the other ranks for most duties up to about 1904, when they were generally discontinued for Full Dress occasions.

Brown leather gauntlet gloves continued to be worn in Review Order by all ranks until 1908 and short gloves of the same colour were retained for Undress until 1914.

On formation, blue and yellow folding field service caps were issued throughout but these were speedily replaced in 1902 by the new peaked staff pattern. These new caps were blue, with yellow bands and piping and black leather peaks and chin straps for both officers and men.

Fig. 35: Officer's Undress Frock 1901-1914. Note the rank braidings on the sleeves above the plain blue cuffs. The Full Dress frock had yellow cuffs.

Fig. 36: Detail of Badges and Titles on Officer's Shoulder Chains.

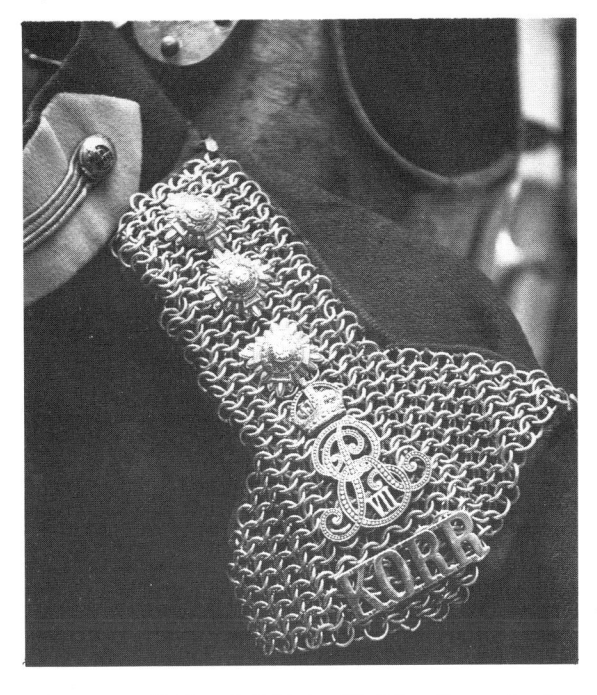

Between 1901 and 1914 the Walking Out order for the other ranks consisted of the forage cap, full dress frock and overalls with Wellington boots and spurs, complemented by the undress short brown gloves and the whip. From 1905, the brown leather waist belt with a shoulder brace and the sword slings buckled together was worn over the frock in this order of dress (Fig. 43).

By the latter part of 1903 a distinctive Full Dress tunic, reserved for Levee Order and attendance at balls, had been introduced for officers. It was therefore necessary to adopt an appropriate gold laced pouch belt, pouch, gold laced girdle and sword slings for wear with the new tunic. The cavalry cloaks were dark blue for both officers and men and the officers were authorised a richly ornamented Mess Dress. There was also a prescribed pattern of mess dress for Warrant Officers, N.C.O.s and men.

Several important changes took place in 1905 in respect of headdress, uniform and accoutrements. Undoubtedly the most significant of these was the exchange of the Colonial type drab helmet for one of Dragoon pattern. The new helmet was black and of slightly Germanic appearance, set off by a striking yellow plume. For all mounted duties the original drab riding pantaloons were replaced by dark blue items with broad yellow cloth side stripes (Fig. 44). For Field or Undress purposes, blue puttees worn with black laced ankle boots and jack spurs were now ordered for all ranks (Fig. 30), and the brown knee boots were exchanged for black ones in Review Order (Fig. 44).

The long Lee Enfield rifle and the Patterson clip equipment for carrying the rifle on the rider's near side were taken into service in 1905. The brown leather waist or sword belt was worn over rather than under the O.R.s serge frock. At the same time, a leather frog and rifle loop were added at the left side of the belt and a supporting strap or brace, carried over the right shoulder, was provided, similar to an officer's Sam Browne belt. The sword slings which were attached to the waist belt to carry the sword when dismounted were retained, buckled together when not required. As a rule, from 1905 in field or drill order, swords were only carried by sergeants and above and attached to the saddle.

When the short lived Patterson clip was dispensed with in 1906, the Mark III Service Rifle Bucket was introduced in its place. This carried the rifle, butt downward, on the off side. The frog and belt loop were now worn on the rider's right and consequently the support brace was transferred to the wearer's left shoulder. From 1906, photographs show that, for a short period at least, the equipment described was worn with the bandolier most exceptionally over the right shoulder and not the left as was customary.

About 1909, the long Lee Enfield rifles were exchanged for the short or S.M.L.E. model and the five compartment, fifty round leather bandolier of the regular 1903 pattern. Orders dated 19 March 1906 give the following information: 'one pair of Blue Serge Trousers (with yellow piping) will shortly be issued to every N.C.O. and Trooper in the Regiment. These will be worn on all Musketry and Stable Parades, on Night Guards and also Fatigue Dress.'

The next changes occurred in 1909 when the brown leather gauntlet gloves were abolished for all ranks and replaced by white wrist gloves which were

Fig. 37: Officer's Mess Jacket 1901-1914, front view. Note the extra embellishment of chain gimp trefoils worn over the cuff by some field officers.

Fig. 38: Officer's Mess Jacket 1901-1914, rear view.

thereafter worn for all Full Dress occasions. The short brown gloves were retained by all ranks for Undress. Regimental Orders dated 15 November 1909 directed that in future officers' dismounted review order would be 'Overalls, Wellington boots, box spurs, dress frock, pouch and gold belt, web sword belt (worn under the frock), gold sword slings, gold sword knot, sword and steel scabbard, white wrist gloves, helmet and plume.' These belts, pouch, slings, etc., were the same as those first brought in for wear with the Levee Dress in 1903. The girdle was not, of course, worn in Review Order, but was still reserved for Levee wear only. The Sam Browne belt was therefore now discontinued for officers in Full Dress and retained for Undress and field dress only. These changes in belts, etc., also applied to mounted review order. The pantaloons and knee boots adopted in 1905 remained unchanged. The O.R.s were also ordered to wear white gloves for review order.

Finally, a most significant change in the uniform of the King's Own Royal Regiment took place between 1911 and 1912, when the authorities at last forced khaki service dress on them. They were the last of the Yeomanry Force to introduce this uniform.

Uniform Details
1901-1914

Headdress.
From 1901 to 1904 a smart Colonial Pattern cork helmet, described by one manufacturer as 'of 10th Hussar shape' was worn by both officers and men for field and full dress purposes. These helmets (Fig. 21) were made of cork covered with a light shade of cotton drill, the peak and edges bound with pale leather. For the yeomen, the pagri or turban was of plain drab folds, whilst the officers were distinguished by a silk pagri of royal blue, comprising about six narrow folds at the top and a single broad fold beneath. The officers had twelve evenly spaced retainer loops of narrow gold braid round the pagri. As a badge, all ranks had the Royal Cypher surmounted by a King's crown over the front of the pagri and for Full Dress there was a dead gilt spike and mount of staff pattern for the officers and a plain brass one for other ranks. When in field or drill order the spikes were removed and a simple drab ventilator button inserted. There were chin chains on drab for review order and plain leather straps for other duties.

Early in 1905 Colonel Barclay had some new sample helmets of the basic 'Albert' or Dragoon pattern (Fig. 22) made up by Messrs Hawkes of London. The front peaks were rounded and the helmets were finished a high gloss black which gave a slightly Germanic appearance. Officers' items were made of aluminium whereas those of the other ranks were of boiled leather. For the officers, the spike and holder and all the other mounts and fittings, including the eight-pointed rayed star front plate and the chin chain holders, were in gilt. The centre device on the star plate, the Royal Cypher and crown, with tripartite scrolls below bearing the title 'King's Own – Norfolk – Impl: Yeomanry' were all in silver. There was no star plate on the other ranks' helmet (Fig. 22), only the crown and cypher badge with title scrolls. All the other fittings, mounts, spike, holder, chin chain, etc., were of brass throughout. The crowning glory of these helmets was undoubtedly the yellow horsehair plume worn by all ranks, which gave the King's Own a unique appearance. Royal approval was duly given for the new helmets and in May 1905 Hawkes supplied 22 of officers pattern and 425 of the other type. Photographs taken at the Northrepps Park Camp in this year show that the new headgear had been issued to all except the Band, who still paraded in the old drab pattern. By the following year, the Band also had the replacement helmets. It is interesting to note that examples of officers' helmets bearing GRV cypher badges, dating them c.1911-14, both with and without the title scrolls described above, are known, although the author is not aware of any O.R. pattern helmets with the GR cypher.

Full Dress.
The officers' Full Dress frock was of dark Army Blue serge (Fig 23). It was cut full in the chest with two unpleated outside breast pockets which had three-pointed flaps, each bearing a small gilt button, and there were two similar pockets without buttons

Fig. 39: Officer's Mess Vest, 1901-1914. This richly ornamented vest was worn with the jacket shown in Figs. 37 and 38.

below the waist. Sewn on each side of the collar were yellow gorget patches about 4½ inches long, pointed at the rear ends and with a 3/16 inch blue light above and below the edges of the patch. A loop of gold Russia braid ran along the centre of each gorget with a small gilt button about 1 inch from the point and the edges of the points were traced with Russia braid. The pointed cuffs were fully faced with yellow cloth and there were three small gilt buttons on each cuff at the hind seam. According to the officer's rank, there were from one to six rows of plain gold Russia braid, first edging the cuffs and thereafter in rows following the shape of the cuff and showing a narrow blue light between each row of gold braid (Figs. 31 and 35). There was a pair of shoulder chains on blue backing bearing metal badges of rank, each with the Royal Cypher and crown at the outer ends and, from the end of 1905, the letters 'K.O.R.R.' below (Fig. 36). From 1901 to about 1906-7 the garment appears to have had five gilt button front fastening, with the exception of that of Colonel Barclay, an officer of considerable stature, whose jacket required six front buttons. Later, the six button front fasting appears to have become official for all officers; other variations included buttons on the lower pockets and pleats throughout. There were the usual side vents to the rear of the skirts. With the exceptions noted above, the garment remained unchanged until 1914.

Information about netherwear, boots, spurs, sword and knot and gloves is given in the general notes above.

Officers' Levee Dress, 1903-1914.
Introduced in 1903, this handsome tunic (Figs. 26-28) was something of a hybrid. Although the King's Own were designated Dragoons, the tunic chosen was of Lancer cut and was, furthermore, of a style in use by the regular Lancers between 1857 and 1873. The round cuffs with slash flaps owed more to the Staff or Foot Guards. The tunic was of dark blue superfine cloth, cut as for Lancers and double breasted, with a half or butterfly turned back yellow cloth plastron. The collar and round cuffs were also faced yellow, as were the three pointed flaps on the cuff; there were three gilt buttons on each of the flaps. There was an edging of narrow gold Russian braid around the outer edges of the plastron and similar gold braid outlining the yellow three pointed flaps on the rear skirts, each of which bore three gilt buttons, with two similar buttons at the hips. The collar was edged round the top and front with a row of gold ⅝ inch wave lace; in the case of field officers, a row of similar lace ran round the bottom of the collar and all officers had a pair of silver encrowned Royal Cypher collar badges. The Artillery pattern gold shoulder cords on blue backing bore embroidered silver rank badges, with a small gilt button at the top of each set of shoulder cords. The cuff slashes were edged with ⅝ inch wave lace and there was a row of similar lace round the top of the cuffs; for the field officers there were two rows of 1 inch lace. Yellow piping was

Fig. 40: Other Ranks Full Dress Frock 1901-1914. The collar badges and shoulder chains are missing from this garment but it has the six button front fastening of c.1911-1912.

Fig. 41: Sergeant Major's Mess Jacket c.1902-1914, front view. The dark blue jacket has yellow gorget patches (which lack collar badges) and the cuffs are faced yellow. The shoulder cords are mixed gold and yellow and all the other braid is gold. This jacket bears saddler's trade badges.

featured down the right front tunic edge and round the bottom edge of the garment; there was also yellow piping down the rear arm and back seams in Lancer fashion and the centre vent on the back of the skirts was similarly piped. Two rows of six gilt buttons were featured in front, with a small flat

Fig. 42: Sergeant Major's Jacket *c.*1902-1914, rear view.

button at the bottom of each row to go under the gold and crimson girdle. The overalls, Wellington boots, box spurs, white gloves, sword and knot were as for Review Order.

Accoutrements. From 1903 to 1908, these items were reserved for wear with Levee Order. However, in 1909, with the exception of the girdle, the gold lace pouch belt and pouch and gold laced sword slings were ordered for officers in Review Order in lieu of the Sam Browne belt worn hitherto.

The pouch belt was of 2½ inch yellow morocco leather on which was mounted 2⅛ inch gold wave lace; there was a plain silver buckle, tip and slide and the silver front ornaments consisted of a universal hexagonal picker plate, with arrow pickers and two chains, attached to a rose boss for holder. Between these was placed a special centre plate (Fig. 25(6)) in the form of an encrowned ER or GR royal cypher surrounded by a wreath, with title scrolls below. The pouch box was fitted with a silver flap bearing an engraved leaf design edge; in the centre of the flap was an ER or GR cypher surmounted by a king's crown (Fig. 29). The sword slings, which were of 1⅛ inch yellow morocco leather mounted with 1 inch gold wave lace, were worn from a web waist belt under the Levee tunic (1903-14) or the Full Dress frock (1909-14). The gold lace girdle with two crimson silk stripes was of Lancer pattern on scarlet silk, with three small gold olivets and gold loops at the wearer's left side to fasten (Fig. 28). The sword was as for review order, with a gold knot and steel scabbard. White wrist gloves, overalls and Wellington boots with box spurs were worn.

Other Ranks Full Dress.
A close study of many photographs from both the Regimental and various private collections taken between 1901 and 1914 reveals numerous variations in some features of the Full Dress frocks of the N.C.O.s and men. These concern the shape of the pocket flaps, the use of pleats thereon and the number of pockets and buttons used throughout. Some of the variations observed by the author are noted here, but there may well have been others.

The other ranks wore a Full Dress blue serge frock very similar to that of the officers (Figs 40 and 43), complete with yellow gorget patches and cuffs and the shoulder chains. However, the gorget patches had blue cord centre loops instead of gold and there were Royal Arms collar badges in lieu of buttons. Their pointed yellow cuffs had two buttons at the cuff seam and one positioned immediately above on the sleeve. Sergeants and above had an edging of gold Russia braid to the tops of the cuffs and all N.C.Os' rank chevrons were padded and of gold wave lace on yellow cloth backing, with regimental arm badges worn above by senior N.C.Os. There were two breast patch pockets, each with a button on the triangular shaped flap, although it would appear that W.Os, Permanent Staff and S.S.Ms had officer's pattern three pointed pocket flaps and four pleated or unpleated pockets from a fairly early date. By about 1912, most sergeants seem to have had this arrangement. The other

Fig. 43: The Commanding Officer and Regimental Staff *c.*1911-1912. Colonel Barclay is seated in the centre of the group; he can be distinguished by the white cover to his blue and yellow forage cap and his frock is of the undress type with blue cuffs. The gold aiguilette of his A.D.C. appointment can be seen. The Adjutant, Captain R. N. D. Ryder, 8th Royal Irish Hussars, is seated at his right and to his left is R.S.M. H. W. Pamplin. The R.S.M., together with the R.Q.M.S. and S.S.M.s in the back row wear walking out order, full dress with forage cap but without the sword. Bandmaster Macartney wears his frock coat and girdle.

N.C.Os and privates appear to have retained the triangular flapped, two breast pockets only, style to 1914, but with the addition of pleats to the pockets by 1912-13. From 1901, the coat had a five button front fastening, but about 1911-12 this was changed to six. The shoulder chains on blue backing were worn throughout from 1901 and the badges and letters thereon were similar to those of the officers.

Regimental Orders early in 1905 refer to special musketry badges being introduced, to be awarded yearly and held for twelve months. They were awarded to the best shots of the sergeants, lance sergeants, corporals and privates. The badge was composed of crossed rifles surmounted by a star and surrounded by a wreath of bay leaves and was worn on the left forearm near the cuff point. These marks of distinction were fully described in paragraph 338 of I.Y. Regulations 1903.

Details of pantaloons, overalls, boots, spurs and accoutrements are given under general notes.

Officers Undress.

For the first twelve months after formation the Undress headgear was a folding field service cap (Fig. 34). The body of the cap, together with the tip or inside crown were of yellow cloth; the flaps and small turned up front peak were dark blue and the crown and edges of the flaps had gold braid welts with two small gilt buttons at the front of the flaps. A narrow black patent leather chinstrap was optional. Although, officially, the field service cap was only shortlived, it appears to have been used occasionally after 1902 by officers, perhaps for mess dress purposes; examples are noted even in the 1930s.

Early in 1902, the new staff pattern cap was taken into wear by the officers. It was dark blue with a yellow cloth band and piping round the crown seam. The plain black patent leather peak was braided at the edge with plain gold wire for the field officers, although Colonel Barclay had his peak embroidered with gold leaf design, as for staff (Figs. 32 and 33). The badges are shown in Fig. 25. All officers had a black patent leather chin strap with two small gilt buttons. These caps were worn for all undress purposes from 1902 to 1914 and were also worn with the field or drill order c.1903-c.1911/12 as there was no khaki service dress before this date.

The second or Undress frock was used for all undress purposes including field and drill order

Fig. 44: Private in Mounted Review Order, 1909-1914. This photograph illustrates the other ranks mounted review order from the introduction in 1905 of the black helmet, blue pantaloons and black knee boots. The white gloves were introduced in 1909 to replace the brown gauntlets.

before c.1911-12. It was much the same as the Full Dress garment, although of a rougher blue serge. There were yellow gorget patches and shoulder chains complete, and the pockets and buttons generally followed those on the dress frock. There was one noticeable difference, however, the absence of yellow facings on the cuffs. These were no doubt omitted for practical reasons, although the gold rank braidings were retained over the plain blue cuffs (Fig. 35). Blue serge trousers with turnups, worn with black laced ankle boots were inroduced for off duty camp wear by officers in about 1905. The pantaloons, overalls, boots, spurs, gloves, belts,

Fig. 45: Church Parade c.1913. It is possible to visualise from this photograph how striking the K.O.R.R. appeared when on parade in their black helmets and brilliant yellow plumes. Two officers wearing their gold laced pouch belts and sword slings can just be seen on the far right, to the rear of the marching men.

Fig. 46: Private in Dismounted Review Order, *c.*1913-1914. Note the O.R. pattern helmet plate, six button fastening to the full dress serge frock, method of attachment of the sword and brown leather slings and the extra-long brown leather sword knot.

Officers Mess Dress.
The officers' mess jacket was of the elaborate gold laced stable pattern, as was the vest (Figs. 37 and 38). This handsome jacket was dark blue, with a yellow collar and yellow pointed cuffs. There were silver cypher collar badges and the top and front edge had a row of 1 inch gold wave lace, with a narrow chain gimp round the base. The front and bottom edges of the garment were edged with similar gold lace all round and a pair of gold lace dummies were situated at the rear edge. Down the sword and knot are described under general uniform notes.

Officers Frock Coat.
A plain dark blue regulation frock coat (Fig. 43) was introduced for officers around 1906 for informal wear and such occasions as sports days in camp. It was double breasted, with blue shoulder straps bearing badges of rank, the straps piped round with yellow and a small gilt button at the top. There was a pair of gilt collar badges, two rows of eight gilt buttons in front and four similar buttons on the rear skirts. The blue round cuffs had blue three pointed slash flaps with three gilt buttons on each flap and the top of the cuffs and edges of the flaps were piped with yellow cord. Either the gold and crimson Levee girdle or one of yellow silk with two royal blue stripes was worn with the frock coat. The coat was worn with overalls, Wellington boots and spurs and white wrist gloves, as for review order.

Officers Cloak.
This item was dark blue. Its collar was lined yellow and it had a double row of gilt buttons in front.

Fig. 47: Corporal Trumpeter in Dismounted Review Order, *c.*1914. Apparently the only distinctive features of the trumpeter's uniform were the red, yellow and blue mixture trumpet cords and the trumpeter's arm badge.

left front edge was a row of tiny gilt seed studs. The shoulder cords, which were of Hussar pattern plaited chain gimp, each had a small gilt button at the top and bore embroidered badges of rank. There was a row of broad gold lace edging the cuffs and in some cases field officers had the extra feature of a row of chain gimp over the cuffs forming a trefoil at the point (Fig. 37). A heavily gold laced and ornamented white waistcoat (Fig. 39) completed the kit, which was worn with overalls, Wellington boots and spurs as for review order.

It appears that, about 1911, probably to save the expense of this richly ornamented kit, a plain new regulation jacket was introduced, one or two examples of which have come to light. The blue jacket had a yellow cloth roll collar and pointed cuffs, and plain blue cloth shoulder straps piped yellow and bearing gilt badges of rank. The cuff was edged with narrow gold Russia braid showing a blue light and forming a trefoil over the point. Yellow braid edged the front and bottom of the jacket, which had four button holes on the left and four gilt buttons on the right edge. The GR encrowned cypher lapel badges were silver. The white waistcoat was cut fairly low, with four small gilt buttons, and was worn with a white shirt and collar and a black bow tie. These garments were worn with overalls, Wellington boots and spurs.

Other Ranks Undress.
Field service caps similar to those of the officers except for the gold braid welts (although it is possible that senior N.C.Os had the gold embellishment) were issued to the men on formation. In March 1902 Regimental Orders stated, 'A universal Cap of approved pattern is now being issued; these caps will be taken into use by all N.C. Officers and Men at once, and are to be worn on all Parades, Drills and when walking out in uniform. The field service cap will be kept for Musketry and Fatigue Cap in Camp, etc., and is *not* to be worn at other times.' The new cap was in fact the peaked staff pattern (Figs. 30 and 43). It was dark blue with a yellow band and piping in the crown seam, a black patent leather peak and chin strap held by two small buttons. Badges were as in Fig. 25. This pattern of cap was retained up to 1914.

From 1901 to *c.*1911-12, the other ranks second best or Undress blue serge frock was worn for all drill, field and fatigue duties. It was only replaced by khaki clothing for service dress in about 1911-12. Of rough blue serge, it has the same yellow gorget patches, badges, shoulder chains, pockets and buttons as the full dress and differed only in that, as was the case with the officers, the cuffs on this garment were plain blue. The same variations in the pockets, number of buttons etc. as on the full dress frock seem to have occurred. For the N.C.Os, the chevrons and badges were in yellow worsted instead of gold. The riding pantaloons, overalls, serge trousers, boots and spurs, bandoliers, sword belts and slings, sword knot and gloves were as described under general uniform notes.

Fig. 48: Group of Other Ranks in Khaki Service Dress *c.*1913-1914. These ORs wear the plain regular pattern service dress which finally appeared in the K.O.R.R. about 1911-1912. Note the 1903 pattern leather bandolier and the scout's arm badge of the private seated on the ground.

Other Ranks Mess Dress.
Several specimens of N.C.O.s mess jackets have come to light over the years, including those in the Regimental Collection (Figs. 41 and 42). They are all of the stable jacket variety and are dark blue, with the exception of one in the Regimental Collection, which is in a dark bright blue material. There are yellow gorget patches on the blue stand collars and yellow pointed cuffs. The collar badges are either Royal Arms or cyphers but there are no centre loops as on the serge frocks. In most examples there is a narrow gold Russia braid edging the cuffs and forming a single eye over the point although one has the edging but no eye. There is narrow gold Russia braid edging down both sides of the front of the jacket and round the bottom edge, which forms trefoils in the front corners and a single Austrian knot flanked by two small eyes in the centre of the bottom rear edge. The shoulder cords, which are twisted, are made of yellow worsted cord edged either side with gold Russia braid. The waistcoat worn with this type of mess jacket was entirely of bright yellow cloth and was plain except for a narrow gold braid edging the top and front of the collar opening. It fastened by means of hooks and eyes down the front. Most N.C.O.s chevrons are of the thin gold braid variety with appropriate arm badges, gold and crimson crowns etc. However, one example in the Regimental Collection, which may well originally have been a private's jacket, has

Fig. 49: The Regimental Band, Mounted, c.1906. This is the only photograph known to the author which shows the band mounted. It was probably taken while they were rehearsing for one of the few occasions when they were required to ride. It is interesting to note that no kettle drums appear in view. The bandsmen wear forage caps, undress frocks, drab pantaloons and blue puttees. Band pouch belts may also be seen.

no gold braid edging down the front or on the bottom edge and is fastened by twelve regimental buttons down the front. The pointed yellow cuffs with three buttons have a plain gold Russia edging, as does the yellow collar bearing Royal Arms badges. Twisted two strand gold shoulder cords, each with a small button at the top, complete the embellishment. In this case, the sergeant's chevrons are of wide gold wave lace on yellow cloth backing. It may well be that on promotion to sergeant this N.C.O. retained a rank and file garment. The overalls, Wellington boots and spurs were as for review order.

Khaki Service Dress.
With the exception of a single photograph, taken about 1911-12, which shows a single officer in khaki service dress amongst a group of O.Rs in blue full dress frocks, an exhaustive search over many years, which included a careful inspection of the whole Regimental Collection, has failed to reveal photographs of the K.O.R.R. in khaki uniform prior to the First World War. Fortunately, a fairly recent discovery of several postcard photographs taken at the annual camps of 1913 and 1914, together with a single reference in the Regimental Orders of October 1912 have thrown some light on this subject. It seems fairly certain that khaki service dress was not worn before 1911-12, and certainly not during the lifetime of their Colonel-in-Chief, King Edward VII. The lone officer who appears in the photograph mentioned above wears a plain khaki staff pattern peaked forage cap and a khaki serge regulation frock with a stand and fall collar bearing collar badges, narrow mixture shoulder cords and the prescribed regulation rank and cuff braiding in combination mixture drab worsted. The pantaloons are a light shade cord and he wears brown knee or field boots. This photograph was probably taken the year the khaki uniform was introduced.

The Regimental Orders of October 1912 state, 'Officers will be permitted to wear out their present Field Service Jackets (almost certainly the first pattern khaki with stand and fall collar) and blue serges. Thereafter new ones must be in accordance with amended Dress Regulations (i.e. open collar with shirt and tie).'

From the postcard photographs of the camps at Beccles in 1913 and Holkham Park in 1914 it can be seen that all ranks wear plain khaki peaked forage caps. The officers have adopted the open civilian style cut collar, worn with a khaki shirt, collar and tie; there are bright cap and collar badges, darkish shade drab pantaloons and brown knee or field boots. The Sam Browne belt is worn but the swords are carried on the saddle. Brown leather wrist gloves complete the uniform and khaki cloaks are strapped over the front arch of the saddle. There are no throat plumes on the horses.

Fig. 50: Bandsman Arthur Barnham c.1909-1910. Bandsman Barnham wears dismounted review order but with the red staff pattern cap instead of the helmet and plume. His full dress frock has a five button fastening only. The yellow cuffs show up clearly, as do the brown leather pouch belt and yellow cord aiguilettes.

Fig. 51: The Regimental Band, Dismounted, *c.*1908. Bandmaster Macartney is standing immediately behind the piled bass and snare drums with the Band Sergeant to his right and the Trumpet Major to his left. Note the silver kettle drums with gilt ERVII cyphers and silver crowns. All the bandsmen wear the peaked forage caps, presumably of the all red band pattern. Full dress frocks are worn throughout as are yellow aiguilettes, except in the case of the Bandmaster. Pouch belts are not in evidence.

For the other ranks, plain regulation khaki serge frocks (Fig. 48) are worn with drab pantaloons, khaki puttees, ankle boots and jack spurs. The brown leather waist and shoulder belts have been dispensed with and the 1903 pattern leather bandoliers are worn over the left shoulder. All the men carry their S.M.L.E. rifles in butt buckets suspended on short straps from the offside of the saddle. It is interesting that the rifle sling is worn over the left shoulder and around the body, drawing the rifle slightly across the yeoman's back. In some cases, blue cavarly cloaks are still in service, carried on the front arch of the saddle; in other cases the coats are regulation khaki. The sergeants carry swords on their saddles.

The Regimental Band
1902-1914

A Regimental Band appears to have been formed soon after formation and numerous photographs show them at various camps. Their uniform seems to have followed very closely that of the other members of the Regiment. At first they had the drab helmet and spike, blue serge frock, overalls, Wellington boots and spurs but not the brown gauntlet gloves. The Bandmaster appears to have been distinguished by having an officer's blue silk pagri on his drab covered helmet. All the bandsmen wore plain tan pouch belts with plain pouches or music cases. Between 1905 and 1906 the band were issued with the new black Dragoon pattern helmets with, as far as the author has been able to establish, the same yellow plume as the other members of the corps.

It was a full military band with reed instrumentation. Although silver kettle drums (Fig. 51) and drum banners (Fig. 52) were presented by 1905, the band does not appear to have performed mounted more than once or twice. A former member of the King's Own informed the author many years ago, 'They certainly appeared once mounted, which was on the Royal Review at Sandringham by King Edward VII and King Haakon of Norway on December 1st, 1906.' A photograph probably taken at a rehearsal for this occasion can be seen in Fig. 49, although no kettle drums are on view. As several members were unable to ride and play instruments at the same time, it was necessary to enlist the assistance of some bandsmen from the 16th Lancers, who were dressed in the Review Order of the King's Own for this occasion.

By 1909, heavy plaited yellow worsted aiguillettes worn from the left shoulder had been taken into use by the bandsmen (Figs. 50 and 51). The only other distinctive feature of the band is that according to a correspondent writing to L. E. Buckell in about 1908, they wore 'cherry coloured caps'; presumably this meant crimson or red. In Fig. 43 Bandmaster Macartney wears an officer's pattern frock coat for an informal occasion. Messrs Stones, the regimental tailors, supplied Bandmaster Macartney with the following items (from a list dated 13 July 1907):

1. New Parade Frock Coat.
2. Shoulder straps piped (yellow)
3. Embroidered Arm Badge (Lyre)
4. Gilt Cyphers to Collar (gilt Royal Cypher badges)
5. Gilt Royal Arms on Shoulder Straps
6. Embroidered Cap Badge (gold embroidered Royal Cypher)
7. Yellow and Blue Silk Girdle (yellow with two royal blue stripes).

Fig. 52: Drum Banner. This banner is one of a pair which are in the Regimental Collection at Swaffham, with the kettle drums. The banners are of dark blue cloth with yellow edging and tassels. The cypher is in gold on a light grey ground.